John Ashbery

Titles in the series Critical Lives present the work of leading cultural figures of the modern period. Each book explores the life of the artist, writer, philosopher or architect in question and relates it to their major works.

In the same series

John Ashbery

Jess Cotton

REAKTION BOOKS

For my parents

Published by
REAKTION BOOKS LTD
Unit 32, Waterside
44–48 Wharf Road
London N1 7UX, UK
www.reaktionbooks.co.uk

First published 2023
Copyright © Jess Cotton 2023

Printed and bound in Great Britain by TJ Books Ltd, Padstow, Cornwall

A catalogue record for this book is available from the British Library

ISBN 978 1 78914 391 1

Contents

Ashbery at Deerfield, *c.* 1945.

Introduction: 'Everybody's Autobiography': Writing Against the Confessional Grain

'No one writing poems in the English language', the critic Harold Bloom wrote in the mid-1970s, 'is likelier than Ashbery to survive the severe judgements of time.'[1] Ashbery's innovative, evasive, comic and confounding poetic forms have reshaped, in the later part of the twentieth century, the American poem as we know it. The American poetic landscape would look very different today without his defining presence. He was a poet who, as per the now much-told origin story of twentieth-century American poetry, came from the cultural margins to redefine the shape of its traditions. And yet, in spite of his rise to fame and the distinctiveness of his style, which has been widely praised and imitated, Ashbery continues to be perceived as challenging and difficult; he is a figure who is widely read yet rarely put on university courses. Evasiveness can often be taken for difficulty, and difficulty can look elitist and off-putting. Difficulty is, after all, the defining characteristic of Modernism. 'How to be a difficult poet' was how the *New York Times* presented Ashbery's work in 1977, following his Pulitzer Prize win the previous year for *Self-Portrait in a Convex Mirror*, which catapulted him from a relatively well-known member of the New York School to a canonical place within the American tradition. The wager of this book is that Ashbery's work feels less difficult once we are able to sit with its ambivalences, its contradictions, and to see difficulty as a different way of knowing. His poetry respects our complexity and makes complexity a way of thinking about the paradoxes, the contradictions and the challenges of twentieth-century American life, replete with advertising slogans, comic art, radio tunes, state surveillance and endless performances of character.

Ashbery formulated a vocabulary for his own distinctiveness in his 1968 essay 'The Invisible Avant-Garde', in which he characterizes his own position as one that, while being accepted by the tradition, continually eschews any ready assimilation so that he might retain an avant-garde status in spite of his general cultural acceptance.[2] Given his now-central place within the American canon, this account might be told as the story of twentieth-century American poetry more generally and, in particular, its relation to the avant-garde as well as to the cultural, social and political climate on which Ashbery's work draws and which it, in turn, makes readable. Making things readable – even when they seem most opaque or out of reach – is central to Ashbery's poetry, and what renders it so distinctive. What an Ashbery poem says is only part of the story. Its attentiveness to a variety of different languages, architectures of feeling and clashing idioms makes it more of a vessel of experience than a discrete object on the page. Its capacious pronouns (making intimacy at once more expansive and more quotidian) and the musicality of its registers characterize the way in which we move through the world: the poem is imagined as an extension of modes of sociality and communication rather than as a mimetic object that exists on the page, to be parsed for meaning.

Ashbery was a prolific writer; his style and idiom make his body of work distinctly recognizable and yet the variety of its forms, modes and styles trumps any ready categorization. In part, the ingenuity of his work lies in its camouflage: his work resists assimilation to any one particular identity, style or periodization, nor is it readily quotable. Still lines remain, outtakes from the insanity of daily life, working like electricity through the mind

– 'I'll brush your bangs/ a little, you'll lean against my hip for comfort'; 'we live in the sigh of our present'; 'Puaagh. Vomit. Puaaaagh. More vomit'.[3] The whole immersive experience of reading an Ashbery poem alerts us to the sublime ironies and banal experiences of everyday life; they are 'cold pockets/ Of rememberance, whispers out of time'.[4] The collections that catapulted him to fame, *Self-Portrait in a Convex Mirror* (1975) and *Houseboat Days* (1977), remain his most characteristic and analysed works. They embody a new poetic subjectivity that became definitive in the latter decades of the twentieth century – in an American context at the very least. It is a poetic subjectivity that is expansive, which constantly shifts registers, and which delights in subjecting ordinary language to mistakes and multiple meanings and transforming common idioms into something strange.

The meditative idiom that characterizes these collections became a defining tone of the contemporary poetic landscape, a tone that is at once placeless yet saturated with an idea of Americanness: an all-Americanness read against the grain. These collections foreground the stage-set of the vast, strange, Fordist and post-Fordist American landscape. 'The pure products of America' – some personal, some interpersonal and some atmospheric – intrude upon an Ashbery poem. Ashbery's Americanness is one that is shaped by avant-garde and European traditions; an Americanness that is, consequently, never quite at home with itself, and is thus alive to its comedy, its contradictions, its grand late imperial structures and its bathetic illusions. Ashbery as a reader of the contemporary is one of the themes this book addresses. It attends to his alertness to new media, his ventriloquism of Pop voices and his accommodation of new forms of technology. As Ashbery himself suggested in a 1992 interview on the *Book Show*, his principle was to write 'very democratically . . . to get as many voices and segments of the population into the poem'. If he has an overriding aesthetic concern, he reflects, it is all-inconclusiveness.[5]

Ashbery had an eclectic taste: 'What else is there besides matters of taste?' he rhetorically poses in a mock-interview with fellow poet Kenneth Koch.[6] His taste, as suggested in his Charles Norton lectures, published as *Other Traditions* (2000), is not only eclectic but tends towards the minor. In the lectures, he shows how inconsistency might be understood as a value and obscurity as a position that affords freedom. There are no keys to unlock Ashbery's work (only his writing on other writers' work, which is so often a way of commenting on his own craft), but rather a series of entry points that are often tonal (humour and evasion are consistent parts of his aesthetic) and atmospheric (oppressive climates are met by a clarity of perception and evasiveness of language). Sponge-like, his poetry absorbs different languages and idioms, just as it is alive to the variety of architectures through which he moved, from his New York state childhood to Paris and to the New York City landscape in which, for the longest period of his life, he resided. The work – as he suggests in a posthumously published poem, written in 1993, 'The History of Photography' – evades the critical apparatus for examining literature in the Cold War university, disappearing back into the mirage of reality from which it comes:

> apples hang heavy on the shores of Lake Ontario,
> waiting for that prime moment of
> sharpness in the air, the coming
> of true reality which shall brook no gainsaying,
> the old languid tale of laundry hanging,
> waiting to be sprinkled and ironed, so that some sort of
> maze of sense may be navigated, then folded
> and put away like a deck chair.[7]

Ashbery was a prodigious reader and his library, now accessible at Houghton Library, Harvard University, ranges from poetry and literature to art and film criticism, architectural history, philosophical and religious enquiry, travel literature and cookbooks – references that make their way into his work in playful and suggestive ways. Ashbery was such a polymath that, while his career is defined by its poetic production, these interests – predominately in art and architecture – influence how he conceives of poetical space: hospitable, responsive and transformative. Ashbery was first and foremost a reader – a 'writer's writer's writer', to borrow the phrase that he uses in an essay on Elizabeth Bishop to suggest the fervent admiration that is elicited in readers of her poetry.[8] What Ashbery identifies as distinctive in Bishop's work is its ability to make 'a world that seemed as inevitable as "the" world and as charged with the possibilities of pleasure as the contiguous, overlapping world of poetry' – a reading of Bishop's work that serves equally as a reading of Ashbery's own. This idea of poetical space (which does away with mimesis altogether) allows us to grasp how we respond to an ordinariness that 'triumphs over its prosaic substance'. It allows for the world of poetry and the 'real' world to exist side by side, and for the possibilities of the former to bear on how we conceive of the possibilities of the latter. In other words, in making 'a' world of poetry inevitable, Ashbery's poetry shows how the existing ones might seem a little less inevitable. The dazzling, contingent inventiveness of his work might be seen as gesturing towards these latent possibilities.

None of Ashbery's work exists in a vacuum: it draws upon its own eccentric traditions as well as social and political events and structures of feeling that circulate around each piece of writing. These, in turn, inform the work's own modes of circulation and the evasion of private and public boundaries that trump the confessional framework that dominated the era when Ashbery set out to become a poet. Ashbery has resolutely positioned his own work as apolitical, but that defence is in itself a tactical evasion. While nowhere does it pass as 'political' or 'protest' poetry, it is the evasiveness of its forms that resists co-optation into any one particular programme, thus making the work a 'source of annoyance for partisans of every stripe', as he writes in an essay on Frank O'Hara's poetry.[9] The unprogrammatic nature of the work is hardly incidental to how it intervenes culturally and politically at a time when partisan lines and the work of decoding meaning are heavily scripted, in ways that set out the boundaries of American citizenship and the work of literary scholarship alike. Saying nothing too clearly, especially when it comes to the figuration of sexual encounters – which nonetheless saturate the work – has its own significance in decades that are marked by the censorship of homosexual identity and McCarthy-era repression.

Ashbery moved within the emerging queer communities in downtown New York in the 1950s and '60s, which intersected with vibrant artistic ones, during a period when queerness was seen as incompatible with an idea of Americanness. As the critic Deborah Nelson has noted, Cold War-era anxieties served to illustrate the ease with which 'questions of national security turned into questions about normative gender and sexuality'.[10] The 'Lavender Scare', which proved more vehement and long-lasting than McCarthy's 'Red Scare', sought to police any forms of sexuality that fell outside of the strictly heterosexual. The evasiveness of Ashbery's forms might be read in and through such contexts; the undefinable poetic subject as positioned against the rigidity of definitions that characterize the mid-century American climate of anxious policing and suppression. It is the climate in which so much of his thinking about innocence and psychic violence, sociality and sexuality, emerges.

Ashbery's work reframes, then, what the political means, making it more capacious so that it might also include questions of intimacy as well as questions of the landscape. Ideas of travel and home – or homelessness and Frenchness – emerge repeatedly in his work as a way of reframing how Americanness is mobilized, and its temporal and spatial coordinates are imagined. Because

Ashbery is interested in originality (though not in the conventional sense of the revered Romantic genius, preferring its more eccentric versions), his work is informed by an avant-garde European tradition that accounts, in part, for his own divergences from what looked, when he started writing, like a typical American poem. 'There's an American feeling that if you do one thing, you've got to do that and nothing else,' Ashbery notes in a 1977 interview: 'It goes against my grain . . . Poetry includes anything and everything [a nod to William Carlos Williams's classic text].'[11] In an Ashbery poem the idea of America is refracted through poetic prisms until different variations of Americanness emerge.

There are not only many faces to Ashbery but lots *of* Ashbery: the proliferate nature of his work is like no other twentieth-century American poet. In spite of the two large volumes of collected poems that exist, this material accounts for only a small part of his entire production; his work often seems limitless in both scope and interpretation. In tune with its democractic impulse, the poems are never entirely 'closed works' – but subject to endless revision, and consequently live in various draft forms.[12] Drafts of the poems, as Ryan Ruby observes, often look like varieties rather than simply earlier versions of the same work.[13] The project of collating the poetry remains an epic undertaking, carefully and artfully advanced by Mark Ford's edited volumes, by Eugene Richie and Rosanne Wasserman's collection of his French translations, and by Emily Skillings' work on his posthumous late writings. Comprehension and completion is something that Ashbery's own poetic system, nonetheless, evades, but the advantage of reading the poems collectively and in their various stages is to feel the rhythm and repetition of ideas float through the body of work as they do the mind.

Against the backdrop of the mid-century confessional lyric, which positions the poem as the archetypal space of autobiography, Ashbery's work is disarmingly indirect and digressive in its mode of communication, and indeed it can be hard to locate the exact place that the personal occupies in his work. The following interview exchange is characteristic of Ashbery's ambivalence about the uses of the personal:

Adam Fitzgerald: So the autobiographical approach to poetry doesn't appeal to you, even curiously so?

Ashbery: I resist the idea that a poet can't invent his or her own life, which may or may not coincide with the real one. In my own poetry, there are autobiographical passages, and there are also ones that *sound* as though they're autobiographical even though they aren't. I reserve the right to invent my own life story.[14]

The work might be read as autobiographical to the extent that it stages a performative resistance to such codes of reading, opening them up to new ways of thinking about the relationship between the writer and the work. As Ashbery suggests, rather than mapping poems onto life, his interest lies in the gap between the life and the work, and poetry's ability to create its own life story.

Ashbery opens up autobiography to 'everybody's autobiography', so that the reader can see something in it of their own life; he had his own formula for this method: a 'one-size-fits-all confessional poem' that becomes a way of including anyone and anything into the apparently personal.[15] This model of rendering the writer's personal life unsettles the codes of confession and the relationship between publicity and privacy. It is, as with so much of Ashbery's work, a wry reformulation of the confessional poets' apparently navel-gazing poetics, but it is also deeply serious in its eschewal of the idea that art must necessarily either centre the self or reject it altogether. Not knowing too much about the biography of the speaker or the poet himself, Ashbery suggests, opens up poetry's modes of sociality. Ashbery's place within the avant-garde coterie known as the New York School of Poets is also central to this mode of communicating; a manner that at once presumes knowledge of the 'you' to which it is addressed and makes this 'you' capacious enough that it could be anyone.

Everybody's Autobiography, the title of Gertrude's Stein's 1937 novel, playfully refigures the terms of autobiography by narrating her own life story from the perspective of someone else (as she does, too, in its sequel, *The Autobiography of Alice B. Toklas*). This queer model of autobiography opens the genre up to new modes of telling, making space for the fictional nature of autobiography and thus shifting its mode from one of confession to one of creation, making the reader aware of how life stories are not simply told but are constructed through the stories we tell about them. A queer model of autobiography is less interested in relating a linear life that maps neatly from childhood to adulthood and seeks instead to focus on the gaps and omissions and the sideways developments that put pressure on how identity becomes legible. Queer life stories expose the fiction that is written into autobiographical modes, making apparent how, as Paul de Man writes, 'the distinction between fiction and autobiography is not an either/or polarity ... it is undecidable.'[16] Undecidability – the question of who is speaking, of what something means – is a font of interest and ambivalence in Ashbery's work that points us to what is left out in ordinary conversation. Ashbery foregrounds the intimacies that sustain us and the modes of address that are so capacious as to be indeterminable.

There are many biographical stories that could be told of Ashbery, none of which would be untrue – just as the many readings that his work generates are not incompatible – and yet it seems fair to say that Ashbery will always occupy that strange site of being at once familiar and yet not quite knowable. 'My own autobiography has never interested me very much,' Ashbery mock-confesses. 'Whenever I try to think about it, I seem to draw a complete blank.'[17] Autobiography is, in his estimation, simply less interesting than poetry. Ashbery is nothing if not a slippery biographical subject, and this slipperiness – or, more generously, this evasive ingenuity – ensures that he presents a model of poetic identity that is queer in the sense that it disrupts normative models of accounting for oneself. This evasiveness is an implicit challenge to the reader – we feel ourselves quite literally unmoored, an unmooring that demands new modes of reading that make it harder to locate the work within an existing body of scholarship, thus narrowing the line between poetry and criticism, making the poem its own kind of criticism that does not take any tradition or biographical knowledge for granted. We might consequently 'think twice before crossing critical pens' with Ashbery, as he writes in his essay on the work of Laura Riding; or, alternatively, we might see how his work can be illuminated precisely in the crossing of critical pens.[18] The version of Ashbery's life presented in these pages should, in this way, be conceived as a portal into the work rather than a definitive decoding tool.

Where to start, then, laying down critical tools: with Ashbery's Americanness, and with the feel of the poem. The poetic landscapes that Ashbery not only details but creates in his poems are expansive, surreal and artificial: French-Midwestern revolving stage sets – poetic spaces that communicate the feeling of living through post-war America – where the question of how to inhabit that space from 'which the fourth wall is invariably missing' and to survive in a world with 'a strict sense/ Of time running out', is the subject.[19] Far from authoritative or didactic in its tone, Ashbery's work often sounds most like the interior worlds inside our own heads, moments marked by play, disinterest, silliness, sympathy, digression, shyness and boredom: they do not police any emotion or see it as incidental to the trajectory of the poem.

Ashbery's astute ear for the idioms of ordinary American speech – what Marianne Moore famously calls 'the plain American which cats and dogs can read' – makes us more aware of the pleasures and absurdities of our own everyday language.[20] Reading Ashbery can seem like daunting work, but Ashbery was also clear that reading should be a pleasurable experience. 'Studious as a butterfly in a parking lot' is how he conceptualizes the role of the poet in his poem 'The Other Tradition': as a kind of distracted attentiveness.[21] Poetry is imagined, as with his fellow members of the New York School of Poets, as an activity that happens amidst the daily business of being curious, bored and variously immersed in the world. In one of his earliest poems, 'The Painter', the subject of the painting, declared by some as Ashbery himself, is revealed as a 'canvas/ Perfectly white . . . At once a howl, that was also a prayer.'[22] This tantalizing image of an artwork so transparent that it defies critical interpretation – allowing nature, rather than art, to usurp the canvas – is one that both endlessly invites interpretation and trumps anything that we could say in excess of the experience that an Ashbery poem leaves on the world.

1

'Living on the Edge of a Live Volcano': Childhood, 1927–42

Born in July 1927 in Rochester, New York, John's childhood was a typically American one: two-parented, rural and conventional. He was the first son of Chester Frederick (known as Chet), a farmer, and Helen Ashbery, a biology teacher. His young life was contained by the farm he grew up on, his junior school and the nearby town of Pultneyville, where his grandparents lived, which was full of cultural artefacts and boasted a prime view of Lake Ontario. It was its own microclimate, as Ashbery explains: 'there is a narrow band along the edge of Lake Ontario where fruit is grown. Just a few miles south the climate and the crops are different . . . even three miles further south', he notes, 'it would not be snowing, while we were up to our necks in it.'[1] This sense of growing up at a remove from the rest of the world infuses his early work. Ashbery's grandparents' home was a refuge from life on the farm, to which he was never quite accustomed: a space filled with books, art and inventions, unlike the Sodus farm, which, during the Depression years, was a space of hard labour.[2] Ashbery describes his father as 'like Johnny Appleseed!', planting fruit trees with his bare hands. Chet's father had owned a rubber stamp factory in Buffalo, and their family story was one of unrelenting seasonal work with diminishing returns. Helen, who Ashbery describes as 'extremely shy', had a different upbringing: she was from the city and her father, Henry Lawrence, who did the first X-ray experiments in the

United States outside of New York City, was a professor of physics at the University of Rochester. Ashbery always felt more at home with the maternal side of his family.[3]

Growing up on a farm, with only one sibling, Richard, and few friends in the immediate vicinity, Ashbery spent much of the summers of his early years picking apples (when he would much rather have been reading) and the harsh, snowy winters huddled indoors, delighting in the discovery of new books – encounters which later made their way into his poems. Ashbery's earliest memories are an assortment of long winters, snowy weathers, fondness towards his grandparents, tenderness towards his mother and distaste for life on the farm and his father's temper. Unsuited to upstate New York rural life, Ashbery retreated to a world furnished by books and films, much to the disapproval of his father. The evasiveness of Ashbery's early work, coupled with its schoolroom setting, might be read in terms of a sensitive child's desire to quell his father's moods – moods that teetered on the edge of rage, aggravated by precarious financial circumstances in Ashbery's early life. While a snapshot might offer a snowy, rose-tinted glimpse of 1930s life in upstate New York, to the young Ashbery, his home life often felt like 'living on the edge of a live volcano'.[4]

In Ashbery's poem 'A Boy', published in his first collection, *Some Trees* (1956), this volcanic paternal rage is imagined as a force that the child speaker tries to hold at bay through a determined evasiveness. This evasiveness depends, the poem suggests, on cultivating a different mode of communication altogether, an equivocation which takes the form of an allusion to the last lines of Samuel Beckett's *Molloy*: 'It had been raining but/ It had not been raining.'[5] Containing two mutually exclusive possible truths, for Ashbery, evocation is not only a way of expanding the alternatives on offer but of resisting the means by which violence takes root. The child in the poem resolves to 'tell 'em by their syntax', using poetic methods to hold off saying anything too directly. A young queer child growing up in a traditional all-American family, evasiveness was a means of survival. Ashbery's grandparents' home provided a welcome alternative to the Oedipal rivalrous structures of the boy–father relationship and a retreat from the models of masculinity that were inscribed in farm life. Even before Ashbery learnt to read, he was fascinated by his grandfather's leather-bound books, which he pored over during visits to their home, where he found the works of Dickens, Thackeray, George Eliot, Huxley, Tyndall, Tennyson, Browning, Jean Ingelow and Shakespeare. Ashbery read Shakespeare from the age of ten or eleven and kept his grandfather's Victorian edition of his plays, which included 'ghoulish steel-engraved illustrations of things like skulls with snakes slithering from their eye-sockets'.[6]

Henry Lawrence owned a set of *The Book of Knowledge*, which Ashbery pored over after school, and his two favourite sections, 'The Child's Book of Poetry' (which contained an array of Victorian and eighteenth-century verse) and 'Things to Make and Things to Do' (full of experiments suitable for children) take on various afterlives in his poetry – most notably in his long poem 'The Skaters' (1964), which revolves around the snowy landscape of his childhood. The childhood referents in Ashbery's work are less autobiographical than part of a culture of childhood to which his later poems allude in their exploration of time, memory, travel and ecstatic experience. The poem is an experiment in memory and writing: 'a puzzle scene' that flickers in and out of sight – as our own childhood does.[7] Until he was about seven, Ashbery lived mainly with his maternal grandparents, which he much preferred since it was in the city and there were lots of children around to play with, unlike the isolation of the fruit farm. After his grandfather retired, they moved to a cottage in Pultneyville, and Ashbery would spend almost every weekend with them. Ashbery's grandparents were his entry point into culture: he remembers being introduced to Kodak's George Eastman when he was about four years old, when his grandfather took him to a reception at Eastman's mansion in Rochester, New York, which is now a famous photography museum. This episode makes its way into his friend James Schuyler's poem 'Dining Out with Doug and Frank', as a digression that reflects on the movement of history:

> By the by did you know
> that John Ashbery's grandfather
> was offered investment-in
> when George Eastman founded his
> great corporation? He turned it
> down. Eastman Kodak will survive.
> 'Yes' and where would our
> John be now? I can't imagine him
> any different than he is,
> a problem which does not arise[.][8]

Henry Lawrence was a much more appealing and friendlier figure than Chet, and Ashbery resembled him physically more than anyone else in the family. He recalls that he had 'this wonderful smell of wool and pipe tobacco – that "old man's smell" that makes Japanese girls faint with disgust'.[9] Ashbery felt 'happily plugged into the Victorian era at their place – which was a happy escape from the continual bickerings at home'.

Ashbery's younger brother, Richard, was born in 1931, when he was three and a half. One of his earliest childhood memories is of his mother coming back from the hospital and his father carrying her up the stairs to her room, 'like a romantic hero, "à la *Gone with the Wind*", though this was long before that movie was made, and my going up to her room after and doing a little dance to entertain her, a sort of jig, I guess'. Ashbery read *Gone with the Wind* in 1942, at the age of fifteen, and this childhood memory seems to provide

Ashbery, far right, with Carol Rupert Doty and Mary Wellington, left, in Pultneyville, *c*. 1930.

the family romance that was otherwise lacking in the Ashbery household. Ashbery recalls this memory alongside the memory of his grandfather coming home in 1932 and telling his grandmother that Eastman had committed suicide.[10]

At a young age Ashbery became an autodidact to amuse himself, and dreamt of becoming a painter. At eight years old he tried – and perfected – his first attempt at poetry, writing a dazzling, precocious poem he titled 'The Battle', about a fight between fairies and bushes. Ashbery was so impressed with what he had written that he decided then and there to stop writing, believing he had already reached his peak. Painting became his central interest at this time: he took a painting class every Friday afternoon at the Memorial Art Gallery in Rochester. Ashbery's painting style – like his diary entries – was marked by a fascination with melodramatic images of femininity and his predilection for nineteenth-century French art.

One of Ashbery's most important early artistic encounters came about through his discovery of Joseph Cornell's *Soap Bubble Set* (1936) in Julien Levy's book *Surrealism* (1936) at his grandparents' house; he recalls feeling moved in particular by an artist who would be, alongside Elizabeth Bishop, a key figure in his interest in a 'homemade' form of Surrealism. Cornell often reveals himself through childhood in a way that is distinctly surreal, a form that becomes the signature of Ashbery's own early work, with its French titles and its revelling in all things childish. In an early poem, 'Business Personals', we find, at odds with the title's purposefulness, the lines, 'The songs decorate our notion of the world/ And mark its limits, like a frieze of soap-bubbles.'[11] This glimpse of Surrealism offered Ashbery a sense in which his world could be otherwise defined – and the role of art in not simply reproducing the world but creating an alternative reality. Reading through Ashbery's copious diary entries between 1941 and 1944, an oblique portrait of the artist as a young man emerges, coupled with an early desire to fashion his own poetic persona.

One of the first entries reads, 'I am writing a theme on my future occupation (artist).'[12]

In his diaries Ashbery not only records his own daily experiences and feelings but notes snippets of conversation that he did not want to forget. The diary was a space where he begun to experiment with a public persona. On Sunday, 20 September 1942, he wrote: 'Today arose about 9:30. Carol and I read and I drew some cartoons which Carol wanted. One was a glamor gal eating breakfast in bed and reading a paper and saying "my God!" . . . A motto – a girl pulling up her hair in front of a mirror, yelling "Hey Myrt, Jean Arthur!" Another two little girls, one saying "I like Walter. He's more the Victor Mature type."' The diary entries are accompanied by marginalia of women's fashion designs. On 7 October 1942, he jots, ironically 'write in my "diary"'. This preoccupation with girlish performance makes its way into another early poem, 'Melodic Trains':

> A little girl with scarlet enamelled fingernails
> Asks me what time it is – evidently that's a toy wristwatch
> She's wearing, for fun. And it is fun to wear other
> Odd things, like this briar pipe and tweed coat.[13]

Ashbery's work – which is constantly returning to 'the mooring of starting out', as he writes in his poem 'Soonest Mended' – is suspicious of beginnings and origin stories, the kind of irresistible momentum that drives family romances and the American pseudo-psychoanalytic narratives that informed the dominant poetics of the mid-century.[14]

Ashbery's early writing is characterized by a playful refusal of the values of maturity that seem synonymous with a heterosexual masculinity. His poetry offers us an image of pre-war life, which is uniquely filtered through his own experience of growing up on a farm. So that, for example, in his two-stanza poem 'This Room', we catch a glimpse of his young self as an oval portrait, where what is 'hushed up' about the past is framed in terms of the violence that is intimated in the odd double passive structure of the lines: 'We had macaroni for lunch every day/ except Sunday, when small quail was induced to be served to us.'[15]

Sketches of women's clothing, accounts of wintry weather, anecdotes from 1930s movies, comic books and early sexual encounters are some of the things we find in Ashbery's early diaries. They offer us a portrait of Little J. A. (to borrow the title of one his early poems, 'The Picture of Little J. A. in a Prospect of Flowers'), which emerges from the precocious interest that the young poet self-consciously cultivates. Ashbery's young diaries provide us, more broadly, with one of the most revealing portraits of queer childhood in pre-war America, interleaving psychosexual revelations with snippets of popular culture and the eccentric 'how-to's' of childhood manuals. The result is an image of childhood not as a developmental narrative but as an artefact created in the interstices of culture; it draws attention to the performances of childhood – Ashbery's and everybody else's – and of the image of the child as poet as we find in the poem 'Hotel Dauphin': 'A child writes/ "La pluie". All noise is engendered/ As we sit listening.'[16] The young Ashbery who emerges in these diaristic takes is a poet-in-the-making who self-fashions himself through his own distinctive tastes and styles. The diary entries are performative and playful, wry and all-knowing; they are continuous with the interest that informs the speakers of his early work who linger at a distance from the experience they recount. Playing the role of the comedian was a way, for Ashbery, of passing the time in the absence of family members, and entertaining friends and family; but also its own defence against the merciless terms by which 'reality' is conventionally defined – a reality that the young poet saw as ill-fitting with his own desires and interests. As Ashbery writes in his senior thesis on W. H. Auden's long poem 'The Sea and the Mirror', 'the only solution' to the reality of a 'false childhood' and a 'false adulthood' is 'seeing ourselves as we are – actors in a completely unconvincing and beautiful drama'.[17]

The beauty of the drama seems dependent, to a certain extent, on its unconvincing nature. In his work, Ashbery creates worlds that are non-mimetic, referring back not to his own experience but to a different means of inhabiting space, one that is, above all, interested in performance. Daily life consists of 'performing the wholly sundry tasks', as Ashbery notes in a 1942 diary entry, in a voice that sounds distinctly unchildlike.[18] Reading young Ashbery often feels akin to leafing one's way through an English comedy of manners novel (exemplified by the work of Ronald Firbank and Ivy Compton-Burnett). Indeed, what we rarely find in the precocious pages of his work is a mood of innocence. In spite of the interest that he takes in childhood as an idea, he appears to emerge fully formed; his young voice feels oddly continuous with the one that we encounter throughout the poet's career: nostalgic about the loss of childhood yet resisting the pull of this nostalgia. Ashbery thought self-consciously about the role of the poet from a young age and he spent his early years cultivating an artistic sensibility. Taking an interest in art and literature becomes a subtle form of resistance to the American life that feels all-assimilable in his youth. Imaginative resources provide a psychological and social armour that allows him to hold off the strictures of identity that are at odds with his own interests and desires, enabling memories of childhood to flood his poems without them suggesting anything in particular about his identity.

In a reading of his work at the American Folk Art Museum in 2002, reflecting on his youth, Ashbery pseudo-nostalgically recalled that, in spite of the hardships of the Great Depression, the 1930s were nonetheless a period when 'You could dress really well for five dollars.'[19] In a 1999 *New York Times* interview with Melanie Rehak, he recalled an early infatuation with his childhood friend Mary Wellington: 'I was fascinated by little girls when I was a little boy, and their clothes and their games and their dolls appealed to me much more than what little boys were doing. Therefore I was sort of ostracized.'[20] References to girl culture can be found throughout Ashbery's early work; it is frequently entangled with his idea of artifice. We hear a 'young girl' speak in the place where we might expect to hear the poet's own childhood self: girlhood provides its own kind of mask. 'Modesty and false modesty stroll hand in hand/ Like twin girls', as he writes in his poem 'Cups with Broken Handles'.[21] In Ashbery's diaries, we often find, accordingly, the all-knowing child entertainer performing a version of childhood and masculinity that enables him to 'pass' as a boy while simultaneously relishing all the ways he does not.

The young Ashbery's distaste for 'boy culture' was measured against Richard, his louder, more gregarious and athletic younger brother. Richard, who had much more of an affinity with Chet, represented the all-American boy that Ashbery was not. Boyhood was something that did not come naturally to Ashbery, and Richard's early mastering of it was felt as a personal affront, showing up his own sensitive, creative and reclusive ways. However, in spite of his athletic disposition and eagerness, in his eighth year Richard fell ill. When his health continued to decline in spring 1940, Ashbery, who was kept largely unaware of the seriousness of his brother's situation, was sent to live with friends and family members, where he occupied himself with stamp collecting, attended art classes at the Memorial Art Gallery and wrote letters to Mary about her duck, Daffy.[22] When it became clear that Richard only had hours to live, Ashbery returned to Sodus, but by the time he arrived on 5 July 1940, Richard had died from leukaemia.

The mourning period that Richard's death occasioned threw a shadow over Ashbery's otherwise unremarkable early life, and references to the brother, whose loss is represented frequently in twin motifs and shadowy doubles, find their way into his work hereafter. The family did not discuss the event of Richard's passing

– just as they refrained from discussing their emotional life more generally – and the atmosphere at home became one of suppressed grief. It seems hardly incidental that in the subsequent years, until 1944, Ashbery would write most prolifically in his diaries. The diary became, in this way, an outlet for what could not be spoken of at home. Otherwise reticent about directly reporting incidents in his own life, Ashbery would reflect on the significance of his brother's death sixty years later, in his poem 'The History of My Life'. Ashbery relates his own life story as one that becomes twain with the loss of his brother, whose premature death thrusts the poet into the future – into a form of solitude and pain that results in the loss of his own childhood. The poem, which opens, in fairy tale mode, 'Once upon a time there were two brothers./ Then there was only one: myself', concludes,

> Then a devouring cloud
>
> came and loitered on the horizon, drinking
> it up, for what seemed like months or years.[23]

The account of childhood that the poem presents is structured not by the before and after of developmental narratives but by the proliferation of various different 'I's that are swept up and consumed by the devouring cloud that descends at the end of the poem. The devouring cloud that emerges might be read as the mourning that descends on Ashbery's horizon: the child's first intimate encounter with death. But it might also be understood, more broadly, as indicative of how we experience time: not as a forward progression but as a static atmospheric mood.

School was a convenient distraction from the impossible work of mourning. Ashbery had, in many ways, a conventional education, but his early autodidactism is central to the ways in which he situates his work and informs how he distinguishes himself from the world that surrounds him. In 1939, in eighth grade, when his English class was instructed to write a true story and read it aloud in class, Ashbery instead invented a fictional story that took the form of a newspaper article – a form of delivery that characterizes both his own and those of his fellow New York School poets' subtle interventions into the scripts of childhood. School – or a resistance to its forms – often seems oddly central to how Ashbery formulates his early poetics, as we find in 'What Is Poetry?' in which the image of school is presented as a place where 'the thought got combed out:/ What was left was like a field.' [24] The poem draws parallels between the restrictedness of schools of poetry and the reductive nature of standardized modes of education. Poetry is positioned as the space that opens up when school is taken out of the equation. Poetical space is central to the affective work that Ashbery imagines poetry can do: 'Shut your eyes, and you can feel it for miles around,' he instructs his readers. [25] The poetic landscape that Ashbery paints in his early work is a markedly Surrealist one, seen from the perspective of an American classroom: the abacus and childish French titles in *Some Trees* might be seen in the light of the young Ashbery's own transfiguring encounter with books and paintings that are distinguished by their hallucinatory clarity, as we find in the opening of 'And You Know':

> The girls, protected by gold wire from the gaze
> Of the onrushing students, live in an atmosphere of vacuum
> In the old schoolhouse covered with nasturtiums.
> At night, comets, shooting stars, twirling planets,
> Suns, bits of illuminated pumice, and spooks hang over the
>   old place;
> The atmosphere is breathless. [26]

Growing up queer and creative in a conventional family, where artistic endeavours were treated with suspicion, Ashbery took refuge in his own academic talents at Sodus High School. He studied French and Latin for two and three years, respectively, and excelled in spelling competitions – a staple of young American life. His early teenage years were also a time of sexual awakening and his diaries are testament to his awareness, at a young age, of his attraction to boys; his anxiety about the discovery of his sexuality informs the coded and reserved forms in which he moves through the world. Although the young Ashbery would, in keeping with the times, come to see his homosexuality as 'aberrant' in his teenage years, his diaries manifest a candidness about his desires – and desire thus becomes co-extensive with creating an imaginary world and literary form in which those desires can circulate more easily (the diary in this way might be seen as prefiguring the importance of the coterie to Ashbery's work). The diary (which he often wrote in French to avoid his mother's intrusions) performs a particular role with regards to his sexuality insofar as it allows him to cultivate a more accepting audience for his work, and a space of play that allows him to experiment with alternative styles of living.[27] In his diaries there are carefully coded references to homosexuality, as playfully suggestive and subtle as the later ones that structure his work, and which contributed to his sense of himself as an outsider figure in small-town America.

Ashbery was delighted when he was asked to appear on the national radio show *Quiz Kids* in December 1941, a desire harboured by evenings in the Ashbery household spent listening to such radio shows. For Ashbery, the quiz provided an opportunity to demonstrate the range of his knowledge (which Chet often challenged by quizzing him on state capitals and statistics from his copy of the *Century Book of Facts*), and he prepared dutifully by spending evenings in the Rochester Central Library reference section, reading up on arcane painters and composers.[28] The show aired just a few days after Pearl Harbor, and much of the half-hour programme was taken up by news bulletins from the Pacific, which 'annoyed [him] no end'.[29] The quiz show presented Ashbery with an opportunity to improve his social stature in town, just as it also occasioned the possibility of escaping the small-town world of Sodus. On his journey to Chicago, where *Quiz Kids* was filmed, he was bought a copy of the *New Yorker* and a Fritzi Ritz comic book – reading material that defines his childhood interests as much as it characterizes his poetry's eclectic range of influences – noting how he feels 'quite distingué' carrying it under his arm.[30] He recalls feeling immediately more mature as the car approached Chicago, as if childhood was measured in terms of perspective.

Ashbery grew rapidly in his early teens, and he took on a comic, slightly lanky figure. In photographs from the period, we see him alternately 'clowning' or retreating from the camera, a device that will become important in the cultivation of his sense of identity. An obscured photographic referent becomes the kernel of the poem that most directly addresses and conceals his childhood self: 'A Picture of Little J. A. in a Prospect of Flowers'. The poem, which alludes to Andrew Marvell's 'The Picture of Little T. C. in a Prospect of Flowers', gives us an oblique autobiographic portrait of the poet as a young child. In the third stanza, the poet is drawn back to his 'small self in that bank of flowers' – an image of his childhood self, and to the stubbornness that he reads into 'this comic version' of himself, which will become a 'virtue' insofar as it provides a kind of invisible shield against the perceptions of others.[31]

Ashbery's 1942 diary was, he notes, purchased specifically for 'literary practice'.[32] In the diaries, which are sometimes narrative and sometimes fragmentary, we get a flavour of the texture of living as a child in the United States through the Second World War. In a 2001 letter, Ashbery recounts the experience of rereading a diary entry from 1941 as entering 'a time capsule' as it moves, as Ashbery's own verse does from the humdrum, to the Romantic sublime, to intimations of violence that lurk just out of the frame:

JOHN ASHBURY

This 14-year-old farm youngster is from Sodus, but he's Rochester's "Quiz Kid." He won that title this morning at the RKO Palace Theater, because he knew two of the three presidents whose first and last initials are the same.

Other finalists in the local Quiz Kid contest were (left to right): James Strachon, 46 Heidelberg, who placed third; Gloria Gerber, 396 Thurston, fourth; Perry Myers, 242 Ormond, fifth, and Charles McHale, 65 Adams, second.

Sodus Farm Boy, 14, Wins 'Quiz Kid' Crown

John Ashbery, 14, Rochester Quiz Kid, is pictured leaving for Chicago last night with his grandmother, Mrs. H. E. Lawrence (center), and his mother, Mrs. Chester Ashbery.

Ashbery on the *Quiz Kids* set at the Merchandise Mart in Chicago, 10 December 1941.

Ashbery with his mother and his grandmother, leaving for Chicago, December 1941.

'A huge blanket of snow fell during the night, but it melted completely during the day.' Dorothy Wordsworth would have approved. The day before, at my art class in Rochester: 'One of my pictures was kept. It was a picture of Nazi boots crushing Holland tulips – "Tulip Time in Holland – 1940."' (And they say I don't have a social conscience!) My other picture was one of a little brook.[33]

The manner in which Ashbery offers up this information – as a wry quip – playfully challenges the perceived ahistorical and apolitical nature of his work. Although violence is rarely an explicit subject of Ashbery's poetry, his body of work – its restlessness and elusivity – is, in part, a way of encoding in his poetry a refusal to be party to violence.

In the poem 'Episode' Ashbery alludes to the feeling of living through historical time: '1937/ was welcoming too, though one bit one's lip/ preparing for the pain that was sure to come.'[34] The imminent pain that lurks on the horizon might be explained, in one reading, in terms of the incipient emergence of fascism that takes place just outside the frame of the poet's childhood. But it might equally be read in terms of the poet's own awareness of the loss of childhood as a stage in which he could revel in a space that allowed for a certain amount of escapism. There was, in the meantime, work to be done. During Ashbery's last summer at home he laboured on the family fruit farm, hammering covers onto cans of cherries, a tedious activity that Ashbery quickly grew to resent.[35] A distaste for work would prove a constant theme but, fortunately, he found a convenient distraction in the figure of a new arrival on the farm: Malcolm White, a seventeen-year-old high school student from Amherst, Massachusetts. Ashbery passed long summer days in the company of White, who was spending the season working on the Sodus Fruit Farm, and their intimacy gave him access to a picture of the romance of homosexual relations, and thus of the possibility of homosexual desire as something that need not be framed as abnormal. Excited about his imminent departure to Deerfield Academy, Ashbery wrote a diary entry mythologizing the end of his childhood: 'Nobody seems to realize but me anyway this is the ending of an era – my childhood,' drawing to a close the contained world that he had known up to his sixteenth year.[36]

2

'Our Days Put on Such Reticence':
The Making of Little J. A., 1943–9

Deerfield, an independent boarding school in western Massachusetts, was a different world to Sodus High School. Boys who attended the academy were prepped for success: it was a through road to some of the elite Ivy League schools. Ashbery immediately reacted with ambivalence to the increasing pressure and strange dynamics of the boarding school environment. His fellow students came from wealthier backgrounds with a much clearer sense of their future path, and while they would raise Ashbery's ambition, it was not an easy transition for a boy who had grown up in a small town in upstate New York. Initially shying away from the more confident types, he spent much of his time at Deerfield anxiously worrying about his social and financial status (only later in life did he learn that a wealthy family friend, whose sons also attended Deerfield, had anonymously paid for his education).[1] Ashbery had trouble acclimatizing to the athletic and social world at Deerfield, and the new tasks and models of masculinity that were demanded of him. Particularly distasteful to him were waiting duties and the task of harvesting vegetables on nearby farms due to the acute labour shortage that was threatening farmers' livelihoods throughout the country.[2] The school's farm programme, which had been expanded through Chet's encouragement, undoubtedly reminded Ashbery of the farm life that he had been so eager to leave behind but which seemed to follow him as he moved east.

Occasionally in Ashbery's work we get glimpses of the legacy of the Great Depression, Franklin D. Roosevelt's New Deal and the rehabilitation schemes that propped up an ailing economy in the 1930s and early '40s. 'Everyone we knew', Robert Gottlieb recalls, 'loved [Roosevelt's] handsome, distinguished face, was moved by his beautiful voice – the famous fireside chats! – and, most important of all in those frightening times, took comfort from the confidence he radiated.'[3] President Roosevelt's famous fireside chats on political and social renovation on the radio, which became a staple of the period, informed Ashbery's view of the political, as Karin Roffman has argued, just as the most residual sense of the effects of the Great Depression resonated in his father's temper – traces that might be read in his poems that take farm life as their subject. Life at Deerfield was, however, for the most part, one of privilege. It would prove an intense intermediary period that bridged Ashbery's childhood and his Harvard years, where he made the intellectual discoveries that would prove so important to his development as a poet. Ashbery's own account of his years at Deerfield is full of an intense anxiety about being liked by his fellow students, coupled with a sense that he might gain the respect he lacked elsewhere through his artistic endeavours. In Ashbery's early diaries, he recounts his initial homesickness at Deerfield and his difficulty acclimatizing to the new pace and challenge of the academic subjects he undertook there. He immediately sought out refuge in 'the library's protecting walls' and in the art studio where his childhood painting classes at Rochester paid off.[4] Deerfield's art teacher, Donald Greason, encouraged Ashbery's work and his painting: a 'still-life of copper pitcher, blue bottom, black backdrop and a basket of yellow flowers', which was an immediate success among his peers, was named picture of the week by Greason in November 1943.[5]

Equipped with his own artistic defences, Ashbery gradually eased into life at Deerfield, making the most of the artistic and

Ashbery, bottom row, far right, *c.* 1944.

literary resources that were on offer to him. School performances, too, provided a space for him to further develop his role as an entertainer. Deerfield's headmaster, Frank Boyden, notes, in a 1944 letter to Chet, of Ashbery's 'very clever' interpretation of the nurse in a school production of *Arsenic and Old Lace*, which '"brought down the house" time after time'.[6] Friendships initially proved difficult for Ashbery, who felt eccentric in an environment where traditional codes of masculinity were entrenched, and where he was constantly anxious, as gossip circulated, that his sexuality might be exposed. A fellow student, Richard Alexander Gregg, known as 'Sandy', noted on Ashbery's arrival, 'Of course he is effeminate and there have been rumors as to his being a homo.'[7] A firm group of Art Club friends proved a necessary bulwark to his sense of isolation, and he forged a firm connection with a new friend, Bill Haddock, who was unusually interested in poetry. Ashbery, however, would later find out that Haddock would prove to be a little too interested in him and had, in fact, started the rumour about him.[8] Although he apologized profusely, it was only the tip of the iceberg. Haddock would prove a slippery figure: first copying Ashbery's homework, then later, at Harvard, Ashbery would find two of his early poems published in *Poetry Magazine* under a pseudonym that Haddock had tried to pass off as his own.[9] Despite this, Haddock, who visited the Ashbery family in Pultneyville in the summer of 1944, proved an important interlocutor for Ashbery, with whom he corresponded about poetry and painting, and talked openly, at least at night, about intellectual ambitions and sexual fantasies (a Buck Mulligan figure of sorts).[10] Haddock, in this way, takes on the role of double (a figure that would feature heavily in Ashbery's early poems) in the story of Ashbery's early success.

Other friendships proved less of a 'sadistic joy'.[11] Gregg, the literary editor of the school newspaper, the *Deerfield Scroll*, was more of an intellectual match for Ashbery. Ashbery impressed Gregg by reciting every single student's home address, and they applied to Harvard together.[12] In one of Ashbery's contributions to the literary magazine, 'A Ride on the Bus' (27 January 1945), he takes as his subject a tense, unspoken family scenario, a portrait of a snowy childhood that reads as an oblique distillation of his own early years, marked by mourning and isolation, observing that in '[the] perfect flakes of snow he felt himself concealed and protected from the accusing eyes of those around him. But the snow was more than a screen; it was a barrier.'[13] Finding a way to communicate and experience the love that becomes the defining subject of the poems he would write over the next couple of years occupied the emerging poet during this period. Ashbery had expected that he would follow other family members in attending the University of Rochester.[14] The prospect of Harvard immediately raised his ambitions, and he spent the spring of 1945 poring his way through modern poetry with a fervour. It was during this period that Ashbery discovered some of the literary figures – Marianne Moore, Gertrude Stein and W. H. Auden – that would prove so important to his poetic development. The intense reading across modern poetry finds immediate expression in his work from this period in which he cultivates a style that combines mysteriousness with a simplicity of address.

In spite of the friendships that he made at Deerfield, Ashbery felt more than ever during this period the sensation of being entirely mysterious; a mysteriousness that becomes central to his poetic persona. In a fictional encounter of his experiences at Deerfield, 'The Daunted', dated 28 June 1948, Ashbery recalls 'Calmly observing the boys around him', realizing 'that he knew their names and where they came from . . . While, I, he thought, being nothing, must always remain a mystery.'[15] The mystery of love and identity is the recurrent subject of the poems that he wrote during this period. This sense of the mysterious nature of private life is also linked to an idea of the possibility of unconscious communication which is, as he figures it in the poem 'Seasonal' (1945), synonymous with a version of intimacy that pushes beyond the conventional definitions of love. Flowers are a recurrent image in Ashbery's work, which are metonymic of the possibilities that poetry affords. The hermetic, tightly constructed poetic worlds of Ashbery's early work provide a kind of refuge and a template for navigating the world outside it: 'Love grows superfluous, and I look at you/ As I would look at flowers.'[16]

Evading processes of naming people or desires is, in Ashbery's work, the condition on which such intimacy is occasioned and, in the process, it transforms the parameters of love. For all his intense private reflection, Ashbery was also during this period intensely conscious of cultivating a public image. In a letter to his childhood friend Mary Wellington, he cast an unfavourable portrait of himself: 'seedy and gangling, with a limburger complexion and dandruff, good-looking only from certain angles in poorly-lit rooms . . . I suppose I'll come out intact,' he quips.[17] A photograph of Ashbery taken in February 1945 gives a more complimentary portrait of the artist, with his brooding stare and slicked-back hair.

Ashbery spent some time in Spring 1945 listening to hours of programmes reflecting on FDR's recent death.[18] In 'Lost Cove', one of several poems that were written during the stay, we find a vision of love that is imagined as a way of being 'less alone in the marshy wood', something sacred and fragile that must be cultivated with the utmost care and attention (a melancholic strain that is later tempered by wit).[19] In the poem, new ideas about intimacy and loss are articulated through the lens of childhood so that 'the child's song, the field in nostalgia' becomes the framework through which queer desire is articulated.[20] The 'lost cove', in this reading, is the childhood world that is never as idyllic – never quite the fictional world – we imagine it to be. Much of Ashbery's early unpublished work wrestles with the need to conceal desires that can only be aired after dark. The poems he wrote at Deerfield give articulation to these ideas, which will later take on a more stylized and concise form in *Some Trees*. Pleasure appears elusive in these early poems, and love is experienced as painful in the face of an absent other. In the poem 'Why We Forget Dreams', we read of the speaker's attempts to place 'the blinding nowhere of your limbs', a 'sad spring lost in my stammerings' in a melancholic account of the lost history of queer love.[21] Sexuality is neither the subject of these poems nor what is concealed, but is rather figured as their whole atmosphere, informing how strategies of communication and feelings are registered and made to seem continuous with the kinds of worlds that poetry opens up in our thinking.

Ashbery's early lyrics position communication as a constant negotiation that is less about what is communicated than the situation that communication establishes. As he notes in an interview, 'I feel that saying something the reader has already known is not communicating anything. It's a veiled insult to the reader.'[22] In this way, Ashbery's poetry formulates a new kind of poetic language that makes the world at once stranger and more familiar – a tendency that he will later characterize as a kind of interior monologue: 'Very often', as he notes in a 1977 interview with David Lehman, 'people don't listen when you talk to them; it's only when you talk to yourself that they begin to prick up their ears.'[23] In an essay on poetry for his senior English class, 'Recent Tendencies in Poetry', written in February 1945, he reflects in a remarkably prescient manner on the complexity of contemporary poetic forms as a response to the marginalized social role of poetry in the period. The essay, which reads like a poetic statement, notes how contemporary poetry – as represented by Auden – is *good poetry*; it is at once 'highly personal and highly original', 'socially responsible' while containing an 'inward enigma'.[24] The argument that is sketched out in the paper demonstrates, contrary to later claims – or indeed accusations – of the apolitical nature of his writing, how the social element of poetry is central to his thinking about what poetry can do. Ashbery concludes the paper by arguing that the next generation of poets, of whom he implicitly positions himself at the forefront, will 'go further in the fascinating and vital occupation of self-expression and self-analysis'. Poetic ambition is apparent in a diary entry, dated 12 February 1944, which reads, 'I will write better poems than I ever have and publish them,' an ambition that would define his subsequent academic pursuits and the burst of writing that he produces during the mid-1940s.[25]

The education that Ashbery received at Harvard was, as the artist Trevor Winkfield puts it, not simply traditionally Ivy League, but one of 'those educations from professors who themselves had received great educations in the 1890s – when as students they were thoroughly disciplined in the Classics and Victorian morals'. Ashbery, as Winkfield surmises, was 'probably one of the last beneficiaries of that approach to life and education. After the mid-Fifties, education became much more "democratic" and open-ended and definitely less strict:' a process that Ashbery's poetry charts in its own thinking about the shifting sands of culture in these years.[26] The Harvard that Ashbery arrived at in July 1945 was one that was marked by the effects of war, which played on in the background during these years: dorms and clubs were closed and many classes had their intake decimated.[27] Military service presented Ashbery with considerable anxiety, and the Selective Service examination did not help matters when he was assigned 4-F status (a classification for mental and physical deficiencies). On 6 August 1945 the USA announced that it had dropped an atomic bomb on Hiroshima. 'Prayer', written shortly after the cataclysmic world event, references the futility of war, the defeat of 'proud lovers' and the failure of agency in the face of an event so destructive that 'The sky broke like an egg.'[28] The last line of the poem mocks the idea of poetry as a force of renewal: 'O send up/ The phoenix from the ashes of a poem.' The childish image of the sky collapsing in on itself reflects the idea, as Paul Boyer argues, that, in the face of a disaster that baffles the psyche, Cold War culture turned to the comic modes of the child's imagination.[29]

Auden was an obvious reference point in these early poems about the futility of war and the violence of patriotism. In March 1946, during his first term at Harvard, Ashbery heard Auden read and felt immediately spurred on to write. Shortly thereafter he wrote 'A Pastoral', which would be published in *Some Trees*. The pastoral becomes a recurrent concern throughout Ashbery's writing that exposes the work that pastoralism does in occluding the reality of violence. 'Just after Ashbery introduces the pastoral image', as Andrew Epstein writes, 'he pulls the rug out from under it, admitting that youth was never rosy to begin with nor were we ever so cozy with our mates.'[30] The landscape that Ashbery presents us with is, on the face of it, however, less pastoral than surreal, and the poem is typical of the collection in setting up a strange relationship between the title and body of the poem. This American pastoralism is, here, infused with violence and the 'license' that 'permeates our deep south'.[31] In a 1976 interview, Ashbery reflects on the pervasiveness of the themes that saturate this early collection:

> As an undergraduate I gave a poetry reading and somebody said, 'Your poems all seem to be about love and death. Why is that?' There are only about three topics in poetry, though I don't know what the third one would be. Now that I have had the unique experience of getting older, which is something I hadn't done when I was young, it seems that this has become my sort of theme. It's nice, in a way, to have a subject, even if growing older is one of the least pleasant things one can do.[32]

The influence of Surrealism was important in this period, opening up a new poetic language that would allow Ashbery to temper his otherwise melancholic tone. Ashbery did not, however, swallow Surrealism whole, viewing contemporary Surrealists as too logical and limited, and expressed his preference for a more 'home-grown surrealism' that he found in Bishop's and Auden's work.[33] In a 1949 university paper on Auden's poem 'Adolescence' – a poem that seems demonstrative of the poetic statement that Ashbery had formulated at Deerfield – he remarks on Auden's witty takes on the platitudes of growing up. Ashbery locates in the poem a manner of writing about past experience that distances the speaker from his own experience, and which encapsulates the 'tremendous mystery and excitement which Auden [here] transmits to the reader'.[34] Much of that excitement comes from an awareness of the shifting lines of the poem, which coincide with the shifting lines of a family history imagined as a map. Ashbery focuses, in particular, on the line 'Dear boy, be brave as these roots,' a tone that seems to echo, or rather foreshadow, Ashbery's 'A Boy'. The portrait of childhood that Ashbery, like Auden, presents is one that is restricted by the demands of conformity and yet is mysterious and unknown. Auden proved a highly influential figure in Ashbery's modelling of his own early poetics, and the appeal of this poem, in particular, seems to lie in its capturing some of the mystery and excitement of teenage years – and the incipient sexuality that informs a view of the world which is strange, messy and inexplicable.

Coming of age in the 1940s, before the term 'teenager' was designated as a definitive stage, Ashbery's own adolescence could be characterized as a period of burgeoning intimacies and of new forms of self-fashioning; a time when he develops his own poetic styles and negotiates his feelings about his sexuality. It gives us, in short, a portrait of what growing up just before the emergence of youth culture felt like, especially to a queer youth who would have revelled in the cultural activities that became possible a decade later (as encapsulated by Frank O'Hara's poem 'Ave Maria'). The late teenage Ashbery had to amuse himself instead with poetry, skipping classes to read his way furiously through modern poets.[35] Through letters, Ashbery kept Gregg up to date with his current assessment of modern poets and declared Auden to be 'the best of all forever and ever'.[36] It was during this period that Ashbery met Kenneth Koch, whom, he reflects, was the 'first poet he ever met'.[37] Ashbery had first read Koch's work in the November 1945 issue of *Poetry*, in which his own poems had been printed by Haddock, and he had been impressed by his work. Their new friendship facilitated conversations about poetry that each had been having independently. Ashbery set the summer of 1947 aside to write, and the result was the publication of 'The Dolors of Columbine' in which Ashbery aligns himself, unlike his Modernist predecessors Eliot and Pound, not with Pierrot, the stock character of *commedia dell'arte*, but with Pierrot's wife, Colombina. An identification with the vacuum at the heart of a 1940s Fordist domesticity is combined with the tone of Wallace Stevens's 'Sunday Morning'. However, as with Ashbery's childhood allusions, the trials and tribulations of femininity are here a mask for the poet to explore the coupling of pain and pleasure that characterized queer sexuality during this period.

After spending a year immersed in modern poetry, Ashbery set out to make his intervention to 'rip [it] wide open'.[38] His friend Bob Hunter declared 'The Dolors of Columbine' Ashbery's 'breakthrough' poem: it certainly develops a level of intimacy unseen in his work up until this point – an intimacy that moves desire from the realm of an idea to an intensely felt experience.[39] In 'The Dolors of Columbine', the self is distinguished by a doubleness, and the poet by the art of performance. If there are obvious Modernist interlocutors in the poem, Ashbery was writing poetry unlike anybody else at this moment. The poem, divided between the fantasy world of its opening and the banality of the poet's daily life, foreshadows Ashbery's insistent situation of the dreamlife and desire firmly within the realm of the everyday. The two-part structure of the poem is characteristic of Ashbery's work insofar as it moves from a solitary reflexivity to centre on the reader: 'the delight/ Of audiences' in whose 'gaze' the poet reads his 'fame', acknowledging how writing, like desire, inevitably and inexorably makes one dependent on others.[40]

Ashbery's reticent embrace of his own desires was felt in an attraction to a new classmate, Frederick Amory, who did not, unfortunately, return his advances.[41] The complexity of negotiating his own feelings is articulated in another unpublished poem that he wrote in 1947, 'My Friends', which could hardly be accused of embracing a rhetoric of the closet: 'Lucky Alphonse, the shy homosexual/ Draws on his gloves in a room full of ferns'.[42] The poem's title is playfully suggestive but it is also demonstrative of how homosexuality tends, as Foucault writes, towards friendship.[43] Poetry becomes, for Ashbery, not simply the space in which desire is expressed, but the form most conducive, as circulated between friends in this proto-coterie fashion, to desire's expression. During the summer of 1947 he began reading Marcel Proust's *Remembrance of Things Past*.[44] In a letter to Jane Freilicher three years later, Ashbery recommends she read the epic work, noting how 'one of Proust's most exciting qualities is the way he demonstrates how circumstances of one's life which seem casual and ephemeral can solidify for the rest of one's life.'[45] Proust's influence can be felt both in the expansive scope of Ashbery's own poetic project, at the level of syntax and, as he suggests, in the importance that is placed on contingent events. Writing his iconic early sestina 'The Painter', the earliest poem to be included in his first collection, *Some Trees*, later that year, he reveals the complexity of his own thought about the nature of art and the elusiveness of his own subject, reaching towards a theory of the poem that dissolves in the act of its own creation.

If Ashbery's later work is often seen as emerging in relation to the artistic currents that dominated the New York School art scene in the 1950s and '60s, his reaching towards a new poetics is, from the start, imagined in conjunction with a painting that is conceived as a kind of prayer to its reader. Allowing his subject to 'remain a prayer' is also a way of refusing the tenets of New Criticism, making a poem that is infinitely more capacious in how and what it could mean. The formal, repetitive structure of the sestina foregrounds the process of the poem over and above its final product, bringing to light, in its quest for 'a painter's moods, or, perhaps, to a prayer', the full irony of this endlessly elusive task – 'getting the sea to sit for a portrait!'[46] The sestina demonstrates Ashbery's own self-consciousness about his development as a poet, which he allegorizes in the poem that evades 'Others [who] declared it a self-portrait'. Ashbery is, in this poem, reaching towards a form of writing that is rooted in personal experience and yet resists pinning down its subject.

The split that Ashbery centres in 'The Dolors of Colombine' is fully articulated in a diary entry of summer 1947 in which he struggles to negotiate 'the triple life which threatens to split at

John Ashbery, *Seaport*, 1948, collage.

the seams any day', negotiating secretarial school, his family home and nights cruising in Rochester: 'the general effect of all this complete unreality; I barely perceive at all.'[47] This position of barely perceived unreality characterizes the position of the speaker in his poems. The experience of inhabiting an unreal world is evoked most powerfully during this time in a series of collages that Ashbery made in his Harvard dorm. The late 1940s were a fertile period for his collages, a form that he would return to in the 1970s and mid-2000s, and collage, both as material and poetic practice, might, in this way, be read as indicative of transitional periods in Ashbery's creative life, allowing him to visually compile a range of different discourses, subject-matters and images in a strangely evocative new language. Take, for example, two that Ashbery made in 1948: the first, 'Seaport', superimposes an image of a raging boy's face over a seaside town, held up by a fish that surfaces from the port; the second depicts two scenes from a children's book of a boy who is attacked by, and then transformed into, a vulture, to the shock of two young girls on their doorstep.

The dream landscapes of these collages are reflected in another poem written in 1947, 'Why We Forget Dreams', which is also a subsection of Freud's *Interpretation of Dreams* (1901), in which he connects the remembrance of dreams to the creative process:

> Total forgetfulness is not serious; but partial forgetfulness is treacherous. For if we then proceed to give an account of what we have not forgotten, we are liable to fill in from our imagination the incoherent and disjointed fragments furnished by memory . . . We unwittingly become creative artists.[48]

If these two collages focus on the subversive undercurrents of childhood – of the childhood imagination as the source of the darkest regions of the psyche – his collage for the *Harvard Advocate* cover (November 1948) recalls, with a twist, a copy of an early Hans Holbein painting that he gave to his mother for her birthday, which was later hung in his parents' living room.[49] The collage features a picture of a series of vases emerging ecstatically from a Greek statue and raining down onto a copy of Holbein's *Anne Cresacre*. The subversiveness of collage as a way of unsettling reality – and of drawing out the unreality of his late teenage years – is here given full artistic licence.

Several weeks later Ashbery composed his signature early poem 'Some Trees', which was published in the *Harvard Advocate,* and written at speed one November evening.[50] The poem, in its mysterious suggestiveness, imagines the entanglement of trees as providing the poet with a new way of imagining intimacy (an image that first emerges in 'Lost Cove'). Part of its disarming simplicity, which derives, in part, from Ashbery's reading of Marianne Moore, lies in how it manages to invoke a tender feeling of love without including the slightest personal reference. Although his teacher F. O. Matthiessen judged that Ashbery was 'more squarely on the mark in dealing with Miss Moore' than with Auden, Ashbery spent the spring of 1949 working on his senior thesis on the latter.[51] The thesis, which focused on Auden's *The Sea and the Mirror,* is in large part a meditation on Ashbery's own emergent poetic practice; a reflection on how a certain level of poetic obscurity works in conjunction with, rather than against, 'the tremendous mystery and excitement which Auden here transmits to the reader'.

In May 1949 Ashbery made perhaps the most definitive encounter of his career when he met Frank O'Hara at a 'small party' held for an exhibition of Edward Gorey's paintings at the Mandrake Book Store in Cambridge, Massachusetts. Hearing a voice across the room that sounded so like his own, he pushed his way across the crowd of animated students to introduce himself. They were not entirely strangers; Ashbery had heard of O'Hara before but, seeing that 'he didn't look particularly friendly' had chosen not to introduce himself. Their encounter proved that was an entirely false appearance: 'after being with him for five minutes', Ashbery recollects, 'you felt you had known him for years.'[52] The friendship that blossomed proved a significant one for twentieth-century poetry. O'Hara was, in his New York years, to be Ashbery's alter ego, a figure whose sensibility came so close to his own that he suspected him 'of being my identical twin', one that Ashbery would often seek to emulate.[53] During the final weeks at Harvard, O'Hara and Ashbery would spend long, languorous days lying on the grass together by the banks of the Charles River, discussing music and poetry. Ashbery was fascinated by O'Hara's knowledge of modern music, and from him he learnt of such composers as Erik Satie, which he was very interested in at the time.[54]

At his graduation, Ashbery, appointed class poet, read one of his old poems – 'A Sermon: Amos 8:11–14' – in which the languages of prayer, homosexuality and promises are brought together in a poetic idiom that advocates a way of travelling 'light/ And lightly . . . Move as water: soon gone . . . Touch nothing long.'[55] A poem which, at first glance, seems arcane, takes on a new meaning in its guise as advice for students (the how-to manual will be Ashbery's most insistent poetic form; poetry in the guise of practical knowledge is the joke and the paradox). The image of desire in motion that is invoked in the poem is characteristic of Ashbery's articulation of ambiguity as its own protection; a way, as he writes, of being 'Sustained in a vast disinterest', a feeling that, as he will find, is also the experience of living in the vast metropolis that he would soon come to inhabit.[56] The distance that Ashbery put between himself and his home life in Sodus entered a new phase as he moved to New York in July 1949, against his father's 'anti-New York' wishes, making a swift exit before cherry season started.[57]

3

'Excitation, Excitation of Feeling/ Excitement, Mental Excitement': The Encouraging Climate of New York, 1949–55

The New York that Ashbery arrived at in 1949 was a city in transition – socially, architecturally and economically. Manhattan was, at mid-century, a city conducive to new cultural forms: rent was still affordable; artistic and queer communities were steadily finding their ground in the fertile zones that the post-war moment opened up. New York provided the kind of environment and readers that Ashbery had imagined in his Harvard years. Gossipy, creative and experimental, the artistic circles he moved within furnished an ideal climate for collaboration. Artists painted portraits of poets; poets wrote poems about painters; and poems were written in the midst of daily (and night) life – while on the telephone, and at work, in O'Hara's famous formulation.[1] Small magazines emerged to provide a form for these creative outpourings. The ones associated with the New York School – for example, *Locus Solus* – were high-brow, conceptual works, while others, like the magazine of the arts *Fuck You*, laid their own irreverence quite clearly on their sleeves, though the distinction between them might be seen as a question of style rather than content.[2]

The communities that New York furnished, and the city's emergent architecture, make their way into Ashbery's writing in less obvious ways than other members of the New York School of Poets, but the excitement of city life, and the coteries he found there, were instrumental to Ashbery's thinking during these years. In his poetry, this influence can be measured by an increasing sense of community and intimacy that enables the poems to assume an implicit reader – rather than having to imagine one: intimacy was no longer out of reach. The poems, as a result, become more playful and humorous, and more comfortable with their queerness. Ashbery was not only brought into contact with the other writers that formed the coterie known as the New York School in these years, but he began to move in circles of painters that included the Abstract Expressionists, as well as figurative painters, such as Nell Blaine, Jane Freilicher and Larry Rivers, with whom Ashbery made friends during these years. This new proximity to the art world allowed him to think of poetry outside of the East Coast establishment that he self-consciously positioned himself against. It is in dialogue with other mediums that Ashbery was able to rethink what poetry might be altogether.

New York was also, for Ashbery, a city with a queer nightlife. Night-time was no longer a space that had to be imagined or reconciled with the strictures of daily life, as in 'The Dolors of Colombine', but was rather co-extensive with the libidinal structures of the city's grid, a grid that was made possible in these years by public contact venues – dive bars, cinemas and the piers – in a democratic urban atmosphere. Ashbery's sexual encounters in this period often take place off-stage, outside of his immediate friendship groups at the same time that those groups are co-extensive with a new, free-wheeling attitude to sexuality that prefigured 1960s youth culture. In the 1953 poem 'White', which documents the anxiety that characterizes the era as well as the new experiences that were unfolding in Ashbery's life, he writes, accordingly: 'Men talk of masturbation in bars/ To shake hands with a strange force.'[3] Friendship is, for Ashbery, too, central to queer experience: 'I am plotting how to spend most of my life amid my friends,' he writes in a 1950 letter to his new friend Jane Freilicher, with whom he shared an apartment on first moving to the city.[4] Moving through New York as a young gay man, Ashbery gained a knowledge of its underground spaces and its shadowy fringes: the transgressions of urban queer life became a way of negotiating the oppressive public/private divide that was central to American experience during these years.

In the work of the New York School, the city is conceived as a constantly changing architectural topography; an architectural provisionality that serves as a model for Ashbery's own thinking about poetic space (as something that should not be too fixed). In an essay on Frank Lloyd Wright he contrasts the 'particularly fragile, vulnerable, and ephemeral art form' of architecture with poetry and painting, arguing, counterintuitively, that 'the greater the architect, the stronger the repressive forces that mean to see

Ashbery, *c.* 1950, photograph by Walter Silver.

to it that his work lasts no longer than a generation at most.'[5] This architectural principle is less overt in Ashbery's work (than it is, say, in O'Hara's, Schuyler's or Barbara Guest's). Yet, the strength of his writing on architecture suggests that his thinking about poetry, and the space that it might culturally occupy, emerges largely in conversation with architectural as much as artistic ideas. Drawing upon the experiments in these fields, he arrives at the conclusion that poetry is, he writes, 'even freer than the visual arts to make up its own universe and then make up the laws that govern it'.[6] The sense of living through a city in transition is central both to the subject and structure of feeling of the energized creative circles in which Ashbery moved. The idea of interior space was, too, opened up by the inner architecture of the tenement building flats that Ashbery and his friends inhabited, providing a different working and living environment to the forms of domesticity cultivated in Sodus, or indeed in his Harvard dorm room.

Ashbery moved frequently during his New York City years: living in motion – a key tenet of his early poetics, which he returns to in his mid-career poems – is coextensive with the rhythm of city life. The early years were characterized by Ashbery's ambivalence towards resuming studies in higher education. Upon arriving in the city, he sublet Kenneth Koch's apartment, a four-storey tenement on Third Avenue in Gramercy Park, and secured a job at Brooklyn Public Library, much to his father's disapproval.[7] If his career as a librarian proved short-lived (lasting only a few weeks), his superior, Richard Elliott, turned out to be an expert guide to the esoterica Ashbery was interested in, introducing him to the writers Jane Bowles and Mary Butts.[8] In the sublet, Ashbery shared a kitchen with Freilicher, who rented the upstairs flat, and who was to become an intimate presence in Ashbery's life and an artistic interlocutor (rather than a muse, as she proved for O'Hara). Freilicher, a 24-year-old figurative painter whom Ashbery described in a letter as 'a pretty and somewhat preoccupied dark-haired girl', was the most important female presence in his life during these years.[9] 'When he and Jane Freilicher meet,' Koch writes in his poem 'A Time Zone' (1990), 'it's as if they'd both been thrown into a/ swimming pool/ Afloat with ironies jokes sensitivities perceptions and sweet swift sophistications.'[10] Ashbery's affection for Freilicher only grew: six years later he wrote, in a letter to Harry Mathews, that she is

> probably my favorite person in the world . . . Also everything she says is screamingly funny, although she doesn't always intend it that way and I am always getting her in hot water by laughing at her gags in the presence of people who don't seem to have noticed any humor going on.[11]

This humour gradually finds its way into Ashbery's work, as does his interest in her paintings.

Freilicher's boyfriend, Larry Rivers, a jazz musician and painter, lived in a loft on Second Avenue by St Mark's where other young painters such as Albert Kresch, Alfred Leslie and Grace Hartigan congregated. Ashbery recalls Rivers as 'the kind of wild and crazy guy we didn't see much of at Harvard', who was 'exciting to be around'. Rivers, for his part, recalls that Ashbery 'would drink to the point where he couldn't stay awake anymore and then wake up and wash his face and go to another party'.[12] It was through Freilicher that Ashbery became acquainted with some of the most prominent figurative painters in the period, including her close friend Nell Blaine. Inspired by his artistic company, Ashbery made a painting of his city view and some new collages, which he sent to O'Hara. A photograph of Ashbery dressed as a Puritan, embracing Blaine at a 1949 Halloween party, appears in a *New York Magazine* article surveying his work in 1991. Ashbery and Freilicher spent New Year's Eve 1949 at a party at Katherine Anne Porter's home. Ashbery welcomed in the mid-century with O'Hara: enlivened by each other's company, they roamed the city for several days.[13]

Jane Freilicher and Ashbery, 1952, photograph by Walter Silver.

Freilicher was, during this period, working on her signature New York City skyline paintings that are offset by a vase of flowers in the foreground. The centring of the flower as an analogy for art might be seen reflected in one of the first poems that Ashbery wrote upon his arrival in the city: his iconic, Surrealist take on his own childhood years, 'The Picture of Little J. A. in a Prospect of Flowers' (see, in particular, Freilicher's 1952 painting *Young Girl with Flowers*). The iconic poem of his childhood, which centres around a child amid a 'phlox' of flowers, it seems, could only be written from the distance that New York life provided; it was published in the *Partisan Review* later that year – a magazine that was home to the New York intellectuals.[14] Ashbery's productivity increased incrementally in this period: '[a] poem a month is about my speed,' he wrote in September 1950, reflecting on the progress of his output that year.[15]

Freilicher took Ashbery along to the set of film-maker Rudy Burckhardt's *Mounting Tension* (1950), which resulted in their performing in the film alongside Rivers and Ann Aikman. The short film is typical of the cinematic and theatrical production associated with the New York avant-garde during the 1950s: improvisational, wry and comical, it takes a light-hearted stance on its own cultural contribution. Both a playful excuse for a collaboration and an innovative experiment, the film unfolds as a send-up of a cultural scene caught up in its mid-century (heterosexual) romantic and (psychoanalytic) cultural obsessions. Halfway through the film we see Freilicher at a desk reading a copy of a detective magazine, with a portrait of Freud in the background and a series of totemic and fetishist objects before her. Freilicher plays the role of Madame Frauhauf, a psychoanalyst and problem-solver who advertises by way of sandwich boards worn by an unhappy-looking young man. The avant-garde performance, in the decade before 'happenings', is characteristic of the cultural scene that Ashbery entered upon his arrival in New York. Rivers plays the part of a patient, whose sexual frustrations Freilicher attempts to resolve at first by Freud's talking cure, and then, failing that, by seducing him. Ashbery assumes the role of the jock boyfriend who has come to Frauhauf for couple's therapy, resentful of the newfound interest of his girlfriend (played by Aikman) in modern art. The scene cuts and the couples have swapped: a possibility that is both a humorous take on heterosexual relations and which seems coextensive with the provisional encounters that are made possible in the city. The actors-cum-artists' familiarity in their daily life with one another and their queering of the heterosexual coupling makes these cinematic productions a natural extension of their friendships – as all forms of collaboration became for Ashbery during these years.

'New York', as Ashbery would later write,

was certainly much cleaner and more agreeable as a city
in the early '50s, when I came here to live, and of course
it was the value of the metropolis that once one was there
one didn't have to think about where one was. One could

think of oneself as living in 'the world,' whereas in Key
West, let's say, one is all too aware of being in Key West.[16]

New York presented Ashbery with the occasion to be present, first
and foremost, without having to navigate a set identity. The fluidity
of moving within queer circles, and being part of improvisatory
cultural networks, created a porousness between his life and his
work that is, in turn, taken up in his poems. In Spring 1950 Ashbery
wrote 'The Mythological Poet', a centrepiece of *Some Trees*, which
is distinguished by a new easiness around the writing of sexuality
and which, in its centring of perverse pleasures, opens up the
question of the poet and the role that he might play in society, a
role imagined as modest and absurd: 'He is merely/ An ornament,
a kind of lewd/ Cloud placed on the horizon,' Ashbery writes.[17]
The poet, for Ashbery, is invisible in the poem insofar as he serves
merely to provide a model or an instrument for experience. In
New York, anything could happen; as Marianne Moore writes in
her poem 'New York', 'it is not the plunder,/ but "accessibility to
experience"'.[18] New York was not simply a lifestyle choice or a place
to live – it opened up new aesthetic possibilities for Ashbery. It was a
place where he no longer needed to write poetry that contemplated
what intimacy might look like in its realized form, but which rather
presented 'accessibility to experience' as the subject of poetry.

Ashbery's new familiarity with the city's space is evident
in 'Chinatown', written in 1954. A reflection on the changes of
Fordist America, it records how 'Dreamy Chinatown' is no longer
a place of the imagination but a part of the city that is the place
you might go to buy fuses.[19] Ashbery's poems, though often seen
as oblique in their subject-matter and eccentric in their taste,
are nonetheless attentive to these new products and processes of
industrialized life. 'Chinatown' might be read as its own response,
or counterpart to, Moore's 'New York': in the poem, Ashbery
reflects on the emergence of new products, on the colonial history

that undergirds the city's foundations and on Chinatown as the place where he goes to disappear, which he describes as 'not an Arp, but a huge Sophie Tauber-Arp/ Burned in the wintry day'. There is a new conversational tone to the poem, a new technique of citation and collage that foreshadows *The Tennis Court Oath* (1962) in this oblique testament to living in New York in the 1950s, which centres an experience of cultural dissonance in its image of 'Christmas, lovely Christmas, descend over Chinatown'. Ashbery read O'Hara's poems with fervour during these early years and they sustained him during periods of uncertainty and depression. On Koch's suggestion, having been rejected from postgraduate studies at Harvard, Ashbery applied to Columbia University's English literature postgraduate programme, which admitted him.[20] In his next move in the city, he found a fourth-floor apartment at 60 West Twelfth Street which he shared with an old Harvard friend, Les Brown, who recalls seeing 'a different man at breakfast with John every morning'.[21]

Although Columbia was uptown, Ashbery preferred life downtown, where 'one could call on friends in the Village', as he wrote in a letter to Koch.[22] Disappointed by the cultural limitations of academic life at Columbia, Ashbery skipped classes and spent his days with Freilicher at the Anglophile Periscope bookshop on East 54th Street, where he could get his fill of the English comedy of manners style of Ronald Firbank, Ivy Compton-Burnett and Henry Green, on whom he was writing his master's dissertation. The only course that seemed to capture Ashbery's attention was 'Classical Drama and Its Influence', taught by Moses Hadas, which prompted the writing of a one-act comedy, *The Heroes*, which was accepted the following year by James Laughlin for New Directions.[23] Ashbery's drama, like his early poem 'Turandot', is even more obscure than his poetry, though it is, in part, a way for Ashbery to think through, in another medium, his relationship to poetry: he writes accordingly of 'the unfamiliarity and the resulting poetry' that arises when we 'get a picture of ourselves'.[24] The play, with its homosexual conceit, was also a space to test out how much camp would pass onstage. As Laughlin would later remark, 'Is it "camp" or what?', a question that lingers around his work. Ashbery, characteristically coyly and evasively, responded – a decade before the publication of Susan Sontag's 'Notes on Camp' – that he would have to ask his friends 'what camp meant'.[25] Ashbery loved performance, but his own plays (he wrote three in total) are far more conceptual than character studies, unlike the more slapstick avant-garde plays that he performed in. They are mostly read as sketches for the poetic innovations that he would devise during this period.

Koch was awarded a Fulbright Scholarship to study in France that autumn, and Ashbery, who had long held aspirations of living in Paris, contemplated a move with greater seriousness.[26] Such aspiration informs the three new poems that he wrote during this period: 'Le Livre est sur la table', 'The Hero' and 'Illustration', which all take up the idea of Frenchness as a way of thinking about a new kind of poetic language. The title of the first poem plays on the idea of a child's French lesson as a playful simplicity and slightly awkward translation, a self-conscious play on his own view that 'Isn't everything good when it's written in French?'[27] Ashbery spent some time visiting O'Hara in Cambridge. Reading O'Hara's new work spurred his own productivity, providing him not only with an ideal interlocutor but a model for a 'freedom of expression', as Ashbery later wrote in his introduction to O'Hara's *Collected Poems*.[28] His looming military anxieties were defused when he received the news that he had been declared 4-F, which made him ineligible for the draft; in response, he noted, with typically wry humour, 'I'll be of far more use to this nation on the home front bolstering the morale of three nervous aesthetes' than he would on the battlefield – a quip that is at the same time indicative of Ashbery's playful relationship to national identity.[29]

For Ashbery, Autumn 1950 was marked by a feeling of 'sterility'. In spite of his general busyness, he wrote in a letter to Koch that 'everything repeats last year, without the vitality of the poetry I read and wrote.'[30] In this spirit he applied for a Fulbright to France, suggesting to O'Hara that they travel to Europe together. In the new year he performed the role of 'John' in O'Hara's Noh play *Try! Try!*, a role that he excelled in, and Ashbery attempted his own O'Hara imitation, 'Incunabula', a reference to Hart Crane's poetic sequence of queer love *Voyages*, an 'exciting forgery' whose baroque construct is tempered by the intimacy that breaks through in its final lines:

> here everything is battered
> but what really intrigues me
> is the way your hair stands on end
> whenever I think of you[.][31]

Subtle references to Crane can be found throughout Ashbery's body of work, as the American poet whose idea of America as a lost Atlantis, drawing on Plato's myth about the cataclysmic destruction of an ancient civilization, is coupled with a critique of all that America leaves in its shadows. At home in Sodus that summer, Ashbery reread Philip Horton's biography of Crane, noting in a letter to Freilicher that if Crane were still alive, 'I'd hold his hand! on the days I wasn't holding Proust's or Firbank's.'[32] The wry comment is a playful acknowledgement of Crane's homosexuality, but it is also indicative of his own desire during this period to locate himself within a queer tradition of poets. Feeling ambivalent about making sexual references overt during this period of repression, Ashbery wrote to Freilicher about his own desire not to be pigeonholed as a queer writer, noting that 'I hate to have people I don't know think of me as one of *those* young writers.'[33] Unsure about how *The Heroes* would be received, Ashbery withdrew the play. A summer of gloom was brightened by a visit from O'Hara to

Sodus, where the two went on a long hike; they contemplated views of Lake Ontario, and O'Hara, in typically flamboyant spirit, went swimming in the lakes.[34]

Ashbery's mood, and New York, drastically improved upon O'Hara's arrival in the city, whose presence had a centrifugal effect that, as Ashbery would later write, 'cobbled it all together'.[35] O'Hara's attitude towards art – making it seem as natural as a telephone conversation – provided Ashbery with a way to think about the role of the artist as a natural extension of social life, something communicative and provisional rather than representative and didactic. Writing was, Ashbery felt, a way of managing anxiety, especially during the period in which McCarthyism took the American imagination by force, first focusing its object on communism (as the 'Red Scare') and gradually enfolding homosexuality (the 'Lavender Scare') as its primary object through which it exerted state control. The post-Second World War moment was marked by the emergence of a vast apparatus for policing homosexuality and yet, paradoxically, it was at this moment that the homosexual came to dictate cultural taste and sensibility – as Sontag would argue.[36] Queer culture has a privileged relationship with a cultural production that is invested in forms of securing the imagination by resisting the apparatus of the enforcement of the state's security.[37]

Ashbery moved into a one-bedroom apartment on 44 Morton Street, an attractive street in Greenwich Village, in autumn 1951. (Laura Riding had lived next door two decades previously.) For New Year's Eve 1951 he held a party with his new circle of poet friends, artists and New York intellectuals. Joe LeSueur remembers meeting O'Hara and Paul Goodman there, while Tchaikovsky's Third Piano Concerto played at full volume in the background on Ashbery's portable phonograph.[38] This period coincided with the start of Ashbery taking up the role of publicity assistant at Oxford University Press. During his days in the office, he came across a

Ashbery, Frank O'Hara and James Schuyler in *Presenting Jane* (1953, dir. Harrison Starr and John Latouche).

battered copy of Iona and Peter Opie's *Oxford Dictionary of Nursery Rhymes* (1951), the influence of which can be detected in two poems Ashbery wrote in this period – 'A Boy' and 'The Pied Piper' – which evoke a dark fairy-tale imaginary and a Surrealist childhood landscape that is continuous with Ashbery's own. The latter of the poems, which opens with an image of a 'half-eaten child' who seems to have been subject to some unspoken damage by 'dark elders', takes on a dark tone, unmediated by Ashbery's usually sardonic play – a predicament that is expressed in the poem's final lines: 'and his notes/ Most civil, laughing not to return.'[39] The darkness of the poem is compounded by the sing-song nursery rhyme, exposing the child's intimate knowledge of psychic violence, just as Opie's anthropological recording of children's playground tunes revealed childhood as an unknown continent.

Another theatrical collaboration was prompted by the arrival of a new member of the New York School, James Schuyler, whom

Ashbery and O'Hara met at Rivers's first exhibition at the Tibor de Nagy gallery in Autumn 1951, and who was back in the city after suffering a mental breakdown that summer. Schuyler, unlike the Harvard crew, had found his way into poetry circles through an acquaintance with Auden and his position working at Kleeman Gallery on 57th Street. Ashbery would be one of Schuyler's greatest advocates and write of the disarming simplicity of his style. Schuyler, in his long poem 'The Morning of the Poem', recalls, in turn, the liberating effect Ashbery had on his own thinking of what poetry could be:

> When I first knew John Ashbery he slipped me
> One of his trick test questions (we were looking at a window
>   full of knitted ribbon dresses): 'I don't think
> James Joyce is any good: do you?' Think, what I did think! I
>   didn't know you were allowed not to like James
> Joyce. The book I suppose is a masterpiece: freedom of choice
>   is better. Thank you, 'Little J.A. in a
>   Prospect of Flowers.'[40]

Schuyler's production *Presenting Jane*, a homage to Freilicher, was filmed in the summer of 1952 by the Broadway lyricist John Latouche at a friend's house in East Hampton, Long Island. The footage of the film is now lost, but stills reveal a sun-washed series of images of Ashbery, Freilicher and O'Hara by an ocean cottage. On the way back from shooting, Schuyler proposed to Ashbery that they compose a novel together to pass the time. The result – *A Nest of Ninnies* – which would preoccupy the new friends intermittently through the next decade, was eventually published in 1969. Ashbery and Schuyler were, in many ways, responding to the collaborative feat of O'Hara's and Koch's collaborative sestina, and collaboration at this stage begins to inform all of their practices. Collaboration is, for Ashbery, not simply a way of producing work, but an aesthetic principle that allows for the writing to be situated within, and continuous with, its immediate social situation. The novel is set in Long Island and New York – and the plot, if it could be so defined, is determined by the trajectory of their journey. Ashbery's and Schuyler's friendship deepened as they felt mutually ignored by O'Hara, who developed a reputation for fickleness during this period.

That summer Ashbery would also become more closely acquainted with the painter Fairfield Porter, visiting Porter's family home in Southampton, New York. The two embarked upon a brief romantic liaison, but Porter, who quickly became fixated on Ashbery, became violent at his rebuttals, resulting in the cooling off of their friendship for a period of six months.[41] Porter's 1952 portrait of Ashbery, slouched on a couch in a tan suit, his face half shielded by his hands, captures the poet in a dejected mood. Back in the city, Ashbery, together with O'Hara, passed the time experimenting with avant-garde theatre. *Everyman: A Masque*, a play that Ashbery wrote while still at Harvard, was presented at the Poets' Theatre

Ashbery and James Schuyler in front of Jane Freilicher's self-portrait, in Walter Mill, New York, *c*. 1968.

in Cambridge in 1951, accompanied by a score by O'Hara. In 1952, the two poets acted in New York's Living Theatre production of Picasso's *Desire Trapped by the Tale*, playing the roles of the two Curtains and the two Bow-Wows. The following year, the Artists' Theatre in New York produced Ashbery's much-anticipated *The Heroes*, which premiered alongside Alfred Jarry's *Ubu the King* that August.[42] *Ubu the King*, which opened to enthusiastic reviews, only ran three nights on account of the fire department's mandate to close the theatre.[43] Jarry's language was seen as provocative, and the homosexual representation on stage that Ashbery feared would end his career undoubtedly prompted nervous reactions (the play would be performed the following year at John Bernard Myers's theatre). Ashbery wrote two poems during this period in which such an atmosphere of anxiety can be felt: the first, 'The Thinnest Shadow', gives a glimpse of the speaker sending up his own depressive state at a remove from daily life: 'A tall thermometer/ Reflects him best,' recalling the alienated puppet-speakers of Eliot's and Bishop's work.[44] O'Hara declared the second, 'Pantoum', with the form's encantatory repetitions of the lines 'Footprints eager for the past' and 'Some blunt pretense to safety we have', 'the most beautiful poem of his career . . . [It] is so serious, it's like a bulb going out.'[45]

Ashbery briefly took up the role of research assistant for the recently set up Council for Financial Aid to Education but felt alienated by its corporate model of education.[46] He was promptly fired from his job and spent his days at home, following the spectacle of the televised Army-McCarthy hearings, which contributed to his feelings of increasing unease.[47] A central premise of the hearings was the question about whether the army and navy had promised the names of homosexuals to McCarthy, increasing Ashbery's anxiety about an imminent draft. Ashbery began visiting a psychiatrist, Dr Frank Hale, who provided the army with a new letter renewing the poet's unfit for draft status, but when he visited the army office, he found that no letter had been recorded.

Jane Freilicher, *Untitled (John Ashbery)*, *c*. 1954, graphite on paper.

Ashbery was subsequently forced to describe the sexual acts that confirmed his homosexuality in vivid detail.[48] Amid this airless climate, he composed two new poems that were included in *Some Trees*: 'Canzone' and 'Album Leaf'. In the former, the possibility of queer communion, imagined by Whitman in the preface to *Leaves of Grass*, is foreclosed by the deadening repetition of 'chill' and the image of 'grass/ Struggling up out of clay'.[49]

The beautifully laconic 'Album Leaf' is another poem in Ashbery's first collection in which the pastoral is a force of violence: 'Sweet peas in dark gardens', Ashbery writes, 'Squirt false melancholy over history'.[50] This series of poems evokes the paralysis of a historical moment that the poet feels acutely, as a young homosexual who could be conscripted into the military at any time when troops were being sent daily to Korea. The crusading national security state impinges itself on Ashbery's psyche at a time of mounting personal anxiety, as Ashbery explains in an interview with Richard Kostelanetz:

> In the early 50s I went through a period of intense depression and doubt. I couldn't write for a couple of years. I don't know why. It did coincide with the beginnings of the Korean War, the Rosenberg case and McCarthyism. Though I was not an intensely political person, it was impossible to be happy in that kind of climate. It was a nadir.
>
> I was jolted out of this by going with Frank O'Hara – I think it was New Year's Day, 1952 – to a concert by David Tudor of John Cage's 'Music of Changes'. It was a series of dissonant chords, mostly loud, with irregular rhythm. It went on for over an hour and seemed infinitely extendable. I felt profoundly refreshed after listening to that. I started to write again shortly afterwards. I felt that I could be as singular in my art as Cage was in his.[51]

The execution of Julius and Ethel Rosenberg added a spectacular dimension to the atmosphere of suspicion that governed the implementation of the federal government's loyalty and security programme. Ashbery, who was applying for jobs during this period, turned to French translation for a breath of fresh air. One of Ashbery's earliest translations – Max Jacob's 'Littérature et poesie' – is a prose poem that centres around a child who imagines visiting Naples; a short work that was, for Ashbery, the most concise expression of the poetic imagination. Jacob's work became the centrepiece for his new translation project, which he made the subject of his fifth application to the Fulbright travel grants, providing him with his long-deferred golden ticket to France.[52]

As a child in upstate New York, Ashbery read French fairy tales voraciously: these stories opened up a new imaginative horizon for little J. A., offering him glimpses of French literature as 'a place of romance and pageantry, and all the things one wants'.[53] The most important early French influence on Ashbery was Arthur Rimbaud, who would become a centrepiece of the translation project. But it was at this time that Ashbery made the discovery of the work of Raymond Roussel, an obscure, eccentric, early twentieth-century French writer who was to have a lasting influence on his own work. Ashbery requested every copy of Roussel's work from a Parisian bookshop, José Corti, on Koch's suggestion, and wrote 'Grand Abacus' under his spell.[54] Roussel's influence on the poem, which also nods to Wallace Stevens's 'Anecdote of the Jar', can be detected in the wandering syntactical lines, which, like Roussel's constantly unfolded parentheses, suggest a referent that is constantly deferred – or lost to history. The children who are conjured in the poem have vanished by the end: the poem flickers into consciousness like a chimera. Roussel had arrived at an artistic formula that Ashbery had already been gesturing towards, especially in 'Le livre est sur la table': a certain simplicity combined with esoteric mystery that makes the poem a world unto itself. In an interview with Rosanne Wasserman and Eugene Richie, Ashbery notes that Roussel's 'illustrations were exactly like the ones I had in a French reader when I was in high school, and the elaborate punctuation was like an exercise in a textbook.'[55] 'What he leaves us with is a work', Ashbery writes in an essay published in ARTnews in 1962, 'that is like the perfectly preserved temple of a cult which has disappeared without a trace, or a complicated set of tools whose use cannot be discovered.'[56]

During the early 1950s the fractious relationship between many of the newly formed members of the New York School was improved by their living with a certain distance from one another. O'Hara's general meanness – which took its toll on Ashbery, dependent as he was on the former's appreciation of his work – is confirmed by O'Hara's admission in a letter to Rivers, that 'last night I was so mean to John Ashbery I could vomit. Sometimes I feel I am some sort of furious friend and can't even recognise myself.'[57] O'Hara was, nonetheless, supportive of Ashbery's new play *The Compromise*, which Ashbery wrote at speed later that spring. At the birthday party of Auden, Auden's partner's Chester Kallman encouraged O'Hara and Ashbery to send manuscripts to the Yale Prize, which Auden had been judging since 1946. The encouragement prompted Ashbery to collate the poems he had written over the past decade into a manuscript, which he titled simply *Poems*, forming the backbone of what would become *Some Trees*. The collections were both rejected in the first round, with the result that they never reached Auden himself. Kallman alerted Auden, who was on holiday in Ischia that summer, and who had not liked any of the manuscripts he had been sent, to ask Ashbery and O'Hara to resubmit their work. Auden, somewhat reluctantly, chose *Poems*. Schuyler wrote in a letter to Koch, later discovered by Ashbery, that '[Auden] didn't think either of them very good, and he chose John's *faute de mieux*'.[58] In the ambivalently praiseworthy foreword he wrote, Auden remarks on the collection's 'calculated oddities as if the subjectively sacred were necessarily on all occasions odd', an assessment that would set the tone of responses to Ashbery's early work.[59]

In May 1955 Freilicher and her new boyfriend, the artist Joe Hazan, and Grace Hartigan and her boyfriend, the photographer Walt Silver, planned a road trip to Mexico, on account of Hazan's need to attain a divorce to marry Freilicher. But it provided the occasion for a typical New York School adventure in an extensive family unit. Ashbery, still desperate to leave the United States and

Ashbery and Freilicher in Mexico, 1955.

thinking that his European tour might be eternally postponed, given the unfruitfulness of his Fulbright applications, decided to join them. Fed up with New York, Ashbery was galvanized by Mexico, which he described as 'staggeringly beautiful'.[60] Six months later, from Paris, Ashbery writes to Freilicher: 'Of course I think of Mexico all the time, and to think of Mexico is to think of Mante. Do you remember also the cathedral there, which was either being torn down or built, and was nothing but a prospect of timbers inside?' He recalls that he had recently seen 'a gorgeous Cinemascope short on Mexico which dwelt lovingly on Mexico City and those skyscrapers that look like toothbrushes. And the Indo-Hispano – will I ever have another poignant memory? To end this tirade, I just wrote a poem which I sent to Frank which is influenced by our ride through mad North and Latin America, one stanza of which is:

Open the car window again! A pretty little scene is going by,
And I want to take a tiny photograph of it.[61]

Wandering around Mexico City, Ashbery found himself in a foreign metropolis that was somewhat like the poetic landscapes of Roussel: Mexico gave him his first sense of being an American abroad. U.S.–Mexico relations were, in the post-war years, at their peak (Hartigan notes in her journal 'an incredibly fast customs inspection'), with Mexico making no attempt to intervene in Cold War politics.[62] Mexico City was, in the mid-1950s, rapidly expanding: its first skyscraper, the forty-storey Torre Latinoamericana, was under construction, and Diego Rivera's murals glorified Mexico's revolutionary history on the city's facades, while the cities of Acapulco and Guadalajara, which the group also visited, preserved an older charm. Mexico, with its colonial architecture, emergent tourist industry and its vibrant sights and sounds, was a feast for young American eyes abroad, a landscape which held a vivacity that would enliven the palette of Ashbery's poems. Hartigan, who records the trip in her journal, recounts the holiday as not only a trip to Mexico but a road trip through the States, which leaves the group with a new impression of what 'America' might be as they pass through mountains and forests, shabby hotel rooms in Virginia and kitsch ones in Nashville, Tennessee.

What they found in Mexico was also a taste of Americana: 'We're all almost delirious with excitement over the newness and the anticipation of Mexico,' Hartigan writes.[63] 'The motel is like a Hollywood B glamour film – I'm half in it and half laughing at it – Giant cheeseburgers, kidney shaped pools, green flood lights,' making note, on the second night, of 'the American Tourist groove' in their room 'like a British Hotel room in Africa'.[64] Hartigan and Silver separated from 'the three J's', who she claimed were after a more 'protected and timid' version of Mexico, on day five.[65] The feasts of impressions that Ashbery encountered on the trip would provide the occasion, upon his return, for the writing of 'The Instruction Manual', the final poem to be included in *Some Trees*, in which the poet is positioned in a bare, clinical New York city office, much like the ones that Ashbery had spent the past three years working at, dreaming of Mexico City. The poem, which positions the poet as an escapist office worker, gives an entirely idiosyncratic portrait of the poet's entanglement with new forms of white-collar work: the poem is both situated in dialogue with, and as an escape from, the literature of the instructional manual. Ashbery had recently taken up the role of copy-writer in the university textbook division at McGraw-Hill; he started to write poetry at the office during the day, in breaks between advertising copy for textbooks, which inevitably resulted in a strange porosity between the two written forms: one technical, the other artistic.[66] The position of working a 'pleasant though ill-paying job', in its typical Fordist mode, while looking out the window, dreaming of another city, becomes the unlikely artistic position from which one of Ashbery's most well-known poems is composed.[67] Poetry gets written, as Ashbery's did, while doing the more menial tasks that pay the rent.

'The band is playing *Scheherazade* by Rimsky-Korsakov,' and the speaker's stream of exclamations make it hard to take him seriously: we are a world away from the performativity and the excruciating anxiety of 'The Dolors of Colombine'.[68] The poem's

Ashbery and Freilicher in Mexico, 1955.

situation from high up in the office block adds a comic dimension to the poet's reveries: as Hartigan notes of Mexico, the humour of the poem emerges from the position of being 'half in it and half laughing at it', a humour that is generous in its self-deprecation while at the same time guarding the value of the reverie; a form that is, as Freud tells us, most indicative of the writer's imagination.[69] Its comic note, in its Whitmanesque spirit, also reads as a sardonic quip at Whitman's constant working through of his own identifications; his sense of being at a remove from the communal world that he imagines in his poetry.

Upon Ashbery's return from Mexico, he discovered that not only had Auden awarded him the Yale Younger Poets Prize (O'Hara had sent a telegram to Mexico but it had failed to reach him) but that the Fulbright foundation had back-pedalled on their decision, after someone had declined the award, and he was granted his long-deferred visit to Europe.[70] 'The Instruction Manual', spurred by this new confidence – and responsive to Auden's positioning of his work – wears its artifice and influences on its sleeve. The final poem of *Some Trees* is, in many ways, Ashbery's self-conscious summing up of his early work. Spurred on by this new turn of events, he set about turning the manuscript into a book, which was published in June 1956 by Yale University Press with a foreword by Auden, who placed his writing within a lineage of poets from Rimbaud to Ashbery himself. Ashbery would spend the next few years reckoning with Auden's assessments of his own work, a working through that takes the form of the collage-like productions of his next collection, *The Tennis Court Oath*. But in the meantime there was France, and the new life it brought with it.

4

'I Love Trashy Things as Long as They're French': Taking French Leave, 1955–64

The France that Ashbery had imagined was informed by the perspective of late nineteenth-century and early twentieth-century writers who strolled down the Paris boulevards. But the post-war French landscape that he found on his arrival in 1955 was in the midst of economic and social modernization and the development of a consumer society. France was undergoing a process of Americanization, which was observed by Lefebvre in the sudden descent of large appliances into war-torn French households and streets following the implementation of the Marshall Plan.[1] The programme prompted France's gradual adoption of a Fordist economy, which, as French economist Michel Aglietta observes, is determined by two commodities: 'the *standardized housing* that is the privileged site of individual consumption, and the automobile as the means of transport compatible with the separation of home and workplace'.[2] The abrupt transformations in home and public space are often imagined in terms of the emergence of objects, a new manifestation that is discernible in the films of the era (evoked most powerfully in the cut-out-like houses, and clinical coupledom in the films of Jacques Tati). Residing in France allowed Ashbery to explore not only a sense of Frenchness but the idea of Americanness from the outside: a way to exist between two languages and two identities. When Ashbery had the opportunity to edit a volume of *Art and Literature*, published by his friend the writer Harry Mathews, at the end of his decade in Paris, he not incidentally asked for a contribution from the French theorist Roland Barthes, whose *Mythologies* (1957) documented the emergence of a new consumer landscape, replete with the cars and toys that transformed post-war French society.

Arriving in one of France's harshest winters, during which snow fell on palm fronds across the south coast, Ashbery had a vision of Frenchness that might well have looked not unlike the cover of his late volume *Hotel Lautréamont* (1992). Ashbery had chosen to be based in Montpellier for his Fulbright award, but he spent the month prior in Paris, which he immediately knew he loved. In a letter to Freilicher he relates how the landscape around Montpellier, where 'one lands in a huge desert full of towering crags', reminds him of Mexico. 'Thyme, rosemary, and lavender grow wild in the desert and make it smell nice.'[3] Ashbery was 'fascinated by the geography of Paris', and would spend his days taking long walks through the city's arrondissements, 'often with some sort of *but de promenade*, such as going to see a Laurel and Hardy movie at some neighbourhood theatre'; he was particularly 'enchanted by their American accents when dubbed in French'.[4] Though Ashbery is known more for his artistic than his cinematic references, he concedes in an interview with Daniel Kane that film 'has probably been more influential' to him 'than visual art': 'I ended up writing about art by chance, really. If I'd decided that I was going to write criticism I probably would have written film criticism.'[5] The avant-garde cinematic forms that were emerging at this moment undoubtedly had an impact on the fragmentary, collage-like poetic forms that he would produce over the next decade. As he later reflects, 'cross-cutting, jump-cutting are certainly things I can recognize in my poetry that come from cinema', noting that he would often 'assuage' his 'taste for all the movies' he missed in the States by going to the *cinémathèque* 'sometime three times a day'.[6]

Ashbery's arrival in Paris was coeval with the emergence of the Nouvelle Vague, a cinematic school that soon became iconic for its subversive aesthetic, fragmented narratives, absurd characters, irreverence for Hollywood and interest in new consumer forms. The cinema was at this moment not only central to French culture but served as a medium through which youth culture expressed itself, in opposition to mainstream views and aesthetics. Cinema was synonymous with innovation; as Georges Perec writes of his young adult characters, 'Above all they had the cinema. And this was probably the only area where they had learned everything from their own sensibilities.'[7] In a January 1956 letter to Fairfield Porter, Ashbery notes that he has recently seen *Ordet* by Carl Dreyer, and 'two movies by the Prévert brothers – *L'Affaire* and *Adieu Léonard*', which 'has the quality of being made up as it goes along – rather difficult to do in a movie.' Three months later he wrote of going to a German film festival where 'really grim and determined cinema maniacs like me bring horrible French sandwiches to the Musée Pedagogique . . . The only great one so far was *Spies* by Fritz Lang which had all the madness and excitement of his early films like *Metropolis* and *The Last Will of Dr. Mabuse* without the lumpy social message which spoils them.'[8] Ashbery's poem 'Our Youth', written during his first years in Paris and published in the December 1957 issue of *Poetry*, is one of a series of poems written in quick succession that explore the meaning of youth culture. An image of disillusioned youth emerges in the collection, coupled with a sense of youth as something that Ashbery was, belatedly, exploring, with greater freedom, in Paris. Ashbery would later satirize the idea of the nineteenth-century 'Grand Tour' of Europe in his poem 'Variations, Calypso and Fugue on a Theme of Ella Wheeler Wilcox' (1969), a brush of satire that also seems directly related to the poet's own youthful exploration:

So my youth was spent, underneath the trees
I always moved around with perfect ease

I voyaged to Paris at the age of ten
And met many prominent literary men

Gazing at the Alps was quite a sight
I felt the tears flow forth with all their might [9]

If ever ready to satirize his own pretensions, Ashbery elsewhere captures the feeling of moving in and out of the life-phase of the teenager – a feeling that is also the poet's own desire to wrestle with the feeling of exile – which emerged as a new stage of intermediary adulthood in the post-war period. The vertiginous feeling of adolescent awakening is evoked as 'velvety pavement sticks to our feet', and in 'Our Youth', the poem is, analogously, 'a room like a bubble, that broke when you/ entered it.'[10] The collection yokes together social and psychic life in poems that insistently and interrogatively chart their own incipient self-awareness.

In Spring 1956, at one of Paris's gay bars, Le Fiacre on rue du Cherche-Midi, Ashbery ran into a literary critic, Henri Hell, who asked Ashbery what he most wanted to do in the city, and his reply was 'to have an affair with a French writer'. They noticed a man who was 'standing nearby, beaming at both of us' and Hell subsequently introduced the man, Pierre Martory, who was indeed a French writer and who would be Ashbery's companion over the subsequent decade.[11] Paris, whose bohemian atmosphere made it throughout the twentieth century a melting pot for queer writers, ushered in a new phase of gay life for Ashbery. In an introduction to Martory's work, Ashbery notes the role of 'Barthes, Foucault, and gay writers' in shifting the taboo that had existed around homosexuality in French intellectual circles, 'an antipathy' which, he notes, had been 'even more pronounced in predominantly left-wing France than it

Ashbery and Pierre Martory, Paris, 1958.

was in McCarthy-era America'.[12] Martory was uncompromising about the representation of homosexuality: asked by his then editor, the esteemed Robert Kanters, to change the ending of his novel, he refused, leaving the work unpublished – a move that resulted in his withdrawal from the literary scene. In 1950s France, sexuality became the subject of intense debate, and homosexuality, while still not legally sanctioned, played a significant role in public life. The increasingly obvious presence of homosexuality in the public sphere – in the publication of novels, press scandals, street cruising and sex work – while prompting a 'moral panic' from certain portions of the right, facilitated for Ashbery a new easiness around sexuality, coupled with the freedom that expat life provided.

If Ashbery had wanted to meet a real French poet, he found one who was more interested in the idea of Americanness than Frenchness (Martory used to say that he loved France but hated the French) and he did not quite fit the 'modernist (or post-modernist) French schools' that were prevalent in the post-war period. When asked in an interview whether Martory was responsible for introducing him to the 'mysteries of French culture', Ashbery responded, 'Yes, but he was also very American oriented. I think he had spent his entire childhood at the movies. He also knew lots of American popular songs – he'd been in the war fighting with the American army in North Africa and had learnt all these songs like "Chattanooga Choo Choo."'[13] Martory – the figure of the French poet that Ashbery had gone in search of – wrote poems with faint echoes of Rimbaud or Char; they were mysterious, laconic, sui generis and resembled Ashbery's own writing. Ashbery and Martory were a perfect match in literary taste as well as sensibility. Although there are few identifiable referents to a real French landscape in Martory's work, a location that surfaces repeatedly is Père Lachaise, the cemetery near where he lived and where his ashes are now scattered, which is also home, to a host of queer writers.[14] In a prose poem written in the 1970s for a book of etchings, it is hard to distinguish between Martory's and Ashbery's voice: 'adolescents listen to the sap rising in them which shall one day flower under these flagstones and don't give a damn'.[15]

A sense of living through Paris's intimacies emerges most forcefully in Martory's 'Prose des Buttes-Chaumont': 'I give you Paris its pairs of eyes its hearts/ Each as big as a boxer's fist/ Listen: they're synchronizing their heartbeats/ In the hum of silence.'[16] Ashbery's relationship with Martory, to whom *The Tennis Court Oath* is dedicated, was a natural meeting of minds: two poets obsessed with each other's cultures and who were interested in witticisms and idiosyncrasies, popular and arcane cultural references, in equal measure. Martory, like Ashbery, as Ashbery notes in an introduction to his translation of Martory's book *The Landscape Is Behind the Door*, shared 'an instinctive French antipathy for criticism mixed with biography and has asked me to keep his life out of this', a model of anti-autobiography that becomes an animating principle of Ashbery's work.[17] While details about Ashbery's life are, in his poetry, too, insistently kept out of the work, the poems that are collected in *The Tennis Court Oath*, nonetheless, return insistently to his meditations on his life stage as a means of reflecting upon beginnings and re-beginnings. In his poem 'They Dream Only of America', written in the summer of 1957, probably on Ashbery's thirtieth birthday (an occasion that he refers to in the poem), which explores Ashbery's complicated relation to the United States in these years, Martory's voice breaks into the poem (as a remark made that day) – 'This honey is delicious/ *Though it burns in the throat*,' a French voice breaking into an American poem.[18] America is not imagined – as in Whitman's poem, which Ashbery alludes to – as a future possibility, but as an impossible dream that can only be realized from afar.

Far from an emancipatory vision of queer politics and utopian horizons, 'They Dream Only of America' concludes with a stark acknowledgement of the co-optation of such revolutionary possibility – 'There is nothing to do/ For our liberation, except wait in the horror of it' – coupled by an admission of intimacy: 'And I am lost without you.' Pronominal shifts are significant in Ashbery's work, and his familiar use of 'they' is indicative of his newfound ease around speaking from within his position of coupledom. Ashbery spent the first few months of his Fulbright taking the train between Montpellier and Paris before relocating to the capital in February 1956, returning there, after a brief period back in the United States, between the summer of 1958 and late 1965. Once based in the city, he was largely dependent on the combined financial support of Martory and his parents, but he was, at least, free from the demands of office work. Ashbery's feel for the city was also informed by the various residences that he inhabited: when he first moved to the city, he stayed at the *cité universitaire* in the Japanese Pavilion, and then in various hotels around St Germain-des-Prés, including the Hôtel Welcome on rue de Seine and the Grand Hôtel de France – rooms that were often unheated and tatty, if not outright derelict. Ashbery was living at the Grand Hôtel, which he recalled had bedbugs, when he met Martory. The couple subsequently shared a *chambre de bonne* in the rue Spontini for much of 1956, which he recalls as nicer and a little bigger than the average *chambre de bonne*, 'with a usable fireplace and a private toilet next to it and a rather lovely terrace'.[19] The rue Spontini also had the advantage of being near a lot of Proustian locations (Ashbery knew all the locations where Proust lived and where his characters had lived, such as Odette in the rue La Pérouse).

Ashbery opens a letter of September 1960 to Freilicher: 'Your letter came yesterday and it is already required reading in my set – Harry Mathews and Kenneth Koch both fell under the table in the restaurant where we all ate last night while reading it.' He gives Freilicher a detailed recommended itinerary to her upcoming trip to Europe, suggesting that she pass through London, which 'is very nice if one doesn't stay too long', and spend four days in

Ashbery in France, 1962.

Rome, where he recommends visiting the Villa Borghese to see its Caravaggios. In Paris, he suggests Freilicher stays at The Pont Royal, 'the best hotel on the Left Bank (which is of course more fun than the Right Bank; Frank O'Hara has always found it very cozy).'[20] Although Ashbery managed to travel widely while in Europe, making his first trip to England in March 1956, and travelling several times to Italy, he made little income during his first years in France, when he subsisted largely by translating a couple of French detective novels and writing articles for *ArtNews*. When he returned from New York in 1958, ostensibly to undertake a doctorate on Raymond Roussel, he stayed with Martory in Harry Mathews's apartment in the 14th arrondissement, on rue Alfred-Durand-Claye who, as Ashbery wryly notes, 'was apparently a renowned sanitation engineer, but certainly hadn't done much of his work in that neighbourhood'.[21] They subsequently stayed in another of Mathews's apartments at the rue de Varenne before moving, in January 1961, to a place with 'three tiny rooms, in the back wing of a somewhat posh bourgeois building', through a connection at the *Herald Tribune*, at 16 rue d'Assas, where they stayed until March 1965. It was the same address, as Ashbery notes, that Mabel Dodge, the wealthy American patron of the arts, lived at in 1914. The French years opened up new work possibilities, for the most part as an art critic, which sat far better with Ashbery than his previous office jobs. Writing about art, as opposed to textbooks and manuals, was also, for Ashbery, by proxy, a way of talking about his own work through reflection on contemporary artistic movements and styles.

Back in New York, Ashbery continued to exert a presence even in his absence: as the art dealer Jill Kornblee remembers, 'everybody talked about him as though he were in the room.'[22] Ashbery's intimate presence and poetic stature remained constant through the letters that he sent to his fellow members of the New York School during this period, a correspondence that is full of literary references and replete with camp innuendo: 'I would love to renew our correspondence if you see no objection, as with a little effort we could easily outdo Voltaire and the Marquise de Chatelet,' he writes in a 1960 letter to Schuyler.[23] To Schuyler, as to other members of the coterie, he sent poems and clippings, as well as pages to be included in *A Nest of Ninnies*, which they were still co-writing across the Atlantic, with occasional witticisms about life in Paris ('August is the cruelest month, mixing dead leaves and tourists').[24] The coterie continued to enthuse about one another's writing: 'You are one of America's greatest poets, you know,' he writes in a 1959 letter to Schuyler, 'so why not write bushels?'[25]

In a 1955 letter to Freilicher, Ashbery writes: 'It is odd to miss America as much as one wants to remain in France; it deprives one of any real existence, which of course is hardly noticed in my case.' The presence of his friends abroad makes its way into his poem 'Rain' – as does New York itself: 'The letter arrives–seeing the stamp/ The van/ New York under the umbrella', which are held together by the intimacy of its address. Ashbery wrote the poem after a year spent back in New York in 1957–8, when he was not writing a great deal. 'I build to you every moment,' he writes in the final section, 'in the tepee of the great city'.[26]

Ashbery has said that he imagined the poems in *The Tennis Court Oath* as sketches that he thought he would recycle into something more finished, but felt he actually succeeded in writing in a new way in poems like 'They Dream Only of America', 'Our Youth' and 'How Long Will I Be Able To Inhabit the Divine Sepulcher', which he wrote in Spring 1957, in anticipation of returning for the first time to New York to take a Master's course in French literature.[27]

Though he was happy to be back within walking distance of his friends, Ashbery had difficulty writing upon his return to the United States, missing 'living so happily – despite frequent fights – with Pierre'.[28] Despite his love of the city and the sociability of New York, his objective was to return to Paris – and to Pierre – which he

Ashbery at the Eiffel Tower, Paris, 1962.

did in June 1958. The poems that bookmark this chapter of his life are marked by his reflections on this new era of his life. For Ashbery, the period after his return from New York to Paris was 'a very difficult' one and the 'extreme collage' that he began might be read as a way of negotiating those difficulties.[29]

In the late 1950s Frank O'Hara made a regular appearance in France, as part of his role as curator at the Museum of Modern

Art (MOMA). In mid-January 1959 he spent two weeks in Paris, co-opting Ashbery to help him and Fairfield Porter unpack the works, and act as a translator, for the Paris exhibition of MOMA's international tour of 'The New American Painting as Shown in Eight European Countries, 1958–1959', which he trusted would not be too 'unpleasant or harassing'. O'Hara also requested that Ashbery make a hotel reservation for him on his behalf, remarking playfully how he knew Ashbery liked to keep up his 'influence over various concierges'.[30] Writing to thank Ashbery upon his return home later that month, O'Hara recalls how he thought 'the spectacle of [Ashbery] and Pierre welded inexorably henceforth in friendship with Joan [Mitchell] and Jean-Paul [Riopelle] was indeed a splendid sight.' Noting how sorely Ashbery was missed in New York, especially by Freilicher, who pounded him with questions about Ashbery, O'Hara affectionately said, 'I really should have organized a lecture in Union Square called "News of JA" because I am getting exhausted repeating and amplifying my impressions for each new tear-filled eye and emotion-choked voice.'[31] O'Hara returned to Paris in July, writing immediately upon his return again, to express how he hates 'everything but you two [referring to Ashbery and Martory] and Paris'.[32] In Spring 1960 O'Hara returned once again to Europe in his capacity as curator at MOMA, mounting a significant exhibition of 'New Spanish Painting and Sculpture', for which Ashbery joined him on a tour of northern Spain and southern France, a visit that prompted the writing of 'Leaving the Atocha Station', a poem about the difficulty of communication and translation.

The occasion of the the writing of 'Leaving the Atocha Station' was, like his earlier poem 'Europe', a moving train: a feeling of only grasping the largeness and the complexity of modern life through a series of glimpses; a sensation that Ashbery articulates as 'a feeling that everything is slipping away from me as I'm trying to talk about it – a feeling I have most of the time, in fact'.[33] Inspired in part by

O'Hara's trip to Spain for MOMA, the poem also conceptualizes a new relationship between travel and technology and the poetic forms it engenders. 'Leaving the Atocha Station' imagines a poetic language as an act of disorientation, and it thus summarizes the experiments enacted in the collection – as a kind of meditation on Ashbery's own experience of continual aesthetic secession. The act of artistic secession, and the ability to secede, in particular, from a repressive regime, is articulated in the poem in response to the work curated in the *New Spanish Painting and Sculpture* exhibition. Just as O'Hara noted the 'striking originality and self-sufficiency' of the work, which places it 'in the foreground of the avant-garde' and brings to 'the work itself the excitement of discovery and the vigor of a liberation which has not palled', Ashbery's poem sets out a poetic language that puts a spanner in the work of 'Time, progress and good sense' – the bandwagons of liberal democracy.[34]

'My favorite paintings that I've seen in France', Ashbery writes to Fairfield Porter in 1955, 'are: *The Marriage at Cana* by Veronese, Degas' *Spartan Youths and Maidens Exercising* and Courbet's *A Burial at Ornans*.'[35] On the strength of his criticism, Ashbery eventually got a job at the *Herald Tribune* in 1960, though, as he noted,

> that didn't pay anything but it did open the way to things that did pay. Even after five years in that job I was making only about $30 an article; but they could pay slave wages because there were so many Americans in Paris who were dying for this kind of work. So I really just lived hand to mouth [with the combined support of Martory and his parents].[36]

The art writing that Ashbery undertook in these years documents, for the most part, the work of French artists and expat Americans based in Paris (he has a whole subsection of his published art chronicles, *Reporting Sightings*, dedicated to

'Americans Abroad'). In his essay 'American Sanctuary in Paris',
he observes how the direction of the cultural exchange between
America and France has been reversed: now French artists
and writers were coming to study in the USA. By extension, he
decides to contemplate that unlikely group to which he belongs:
'Americans who still continue to live and work in France', who, 'with
today's communications and transportation', hardly qualify as
'expatriates'.[37] It is from this unlikely position, which is also a way
to rethink his relation to the avant-garde, 'first ahead of it and now
behind it, without everything having gone through an intervening
period of acceptance', that he formulates his own position vis-à-vis
the tradition, recognizing 'the redeeming feature' of this position as
'precisely the inability of identifying anywhere'.[38]

Ashbery's primary model for this mode of dis-identification
from American life, which also allowed him to get at the sense of
feeling 'intensely American', was Gertrude Stein, whose legendary
queer literary salon in Paris was the space around which so
many early artists and writers gathered in the first decades of the
twentieth century.[39] In a 1971 review of her work, he reflects on how
'the distance from America afforded the proper focus and even the
occasion for a monumental study of *The Making of the Americans*;
the foreign language that surrounded her was probably also a
necessary insulation for the immense effort of concentration that
this book required'.[40] As is often the case, Ashbery's commentary
on another writer's practice, as he suggests of Stein in his opening,
is an opportunity to reflect on his own practice and to situate his
writing within a lineage that gets at the 'neutral atmosphere of Paris
– stilted and *arrière-garde* on the one hand,' he writes, 'teeming with
unrecognized artistic ferment on the other'.[41] *The Tennis Court Oath*
might be considered, accordingly, as Ashbery's own *The Making of
the Americans*. The idea of constructing a neutral language in the
collection was achieved, in part, through situating the poem in
the act of translation between French and English. But it was also

a position that had been formulated contemporaneously by the New Realists, an emergent school of visual artists who provided a counterpart to the American assemblages of Robert Rauschenberg and Jasper Johns, which lasted roughly from 1960 to 1963.

Responding in an interview with Mark Ford, published in 2003, to whether art reviews helped his poetry, Ashbery points to the emergence of a new level of productivity, noting that 'having to be chained to a typewriter and turn out an article twice a week caused me, at one point, to wonder, "Why can't I write poetry this way to meet my own deadlines instead of somebody else's?"'[42] It was at this point that he began writing poems on a typewriter, which encouraged a new expansiveness: 'writing such long lines I'd forget the end before I got to it'.[43] The collage-like logic of *The Tennis Court Oath* makes it the most controversial of Ashbery's collections, and indeed its largely negative first reviews correspond with his own hesitancy over the collection.

In his Robert Frost Medal Address, Ashbery notes how his writing during this period was also a taking stock of how much 'spoken American language, thanks to Auden's example of the colloquial, entered into my writing', noting how 'Thoughts of a Young Girl' 'has in recent years found favour with me that it didn't have originally'.[44] The two-part poem, the first poem Ashbery wrote upon arriving in Paris, takes the form of a French conversation lesson. Drawing upon a French fairy tale imaginary (of Rumpelstiltskin in particular, but also of the kind he was translating around this time), it plays on the disjunction between French and English, between an American plainness and a French artifice, the former of which tempers the latter in Ashbery's work. Ashbery was, undoubtedly, reflecting on his new immersion in French culture – the possibilities and constraints that were opened up by expatriate social and cultural life – and the dwarf's imagining of the girl's artifice is, in part, a reflection on the new poetic imaginaries that Paris opened up for him.

Ashbery notes the 'state of restless experimenting' that followed over the 'next two or three years'.[45] This period of writing was informed by visits to the American Library in Paris, where he would 'leaf through popular magazines, looking for a tone of voice [he] felt was lacking' or he would 'buy magazines like *Esquire* and look through them, copying down random bits of phrases in a sort of collage technique – unaware that about the same time Burroughs, Allen Ginsberg and Gregory Corso were practicing doing "cut ups" elsewhere in Paris'.[46] Ashbery remarks on the 'odd coincidence that we all happened on this way of making writing at this particular time and place', suggesting that it might be read as a reaction to a particular climate as opposed to a model of influence.

While he saw many of the poems as experiments, there were a few in which he thought he had 'achieved a satisfactory amalgam of [his] earlier style', among which he includes 'To Redouté'.[47] Like 'Thoughts of a Young Girl', the poem has a dazzling surface and a lightness that retains Ashbery's subversive humour. 'Others are', he concedes, 'so fragmentary as to defeat most readers,' and he notes the influence of several important musical works including one by Luciano Berio, which he heard on the radio, 'Omaggio a Joyce', in which the composer repurposes Joyce's work, 'stretching out the syllables, cutting and blurring the originals in a way I admired'. Ashbery explains how 'these distortions of beautiful but rather simplistic poetry seemed to get at the heart of what I thought poetry was: one part shimmer, three parts shriek.'[48]

This shimmery shriek is demonstrated most forcefully in 'Europe' (1960), which Ashbery wrote after passing through the Paris Métro station Europe on a moving train: 'Somehow the sight of those ceramic letters set in a tile wall, with hordes of subway passengers passing by made me realize for the first time that I was – Eureka! – in Europe.'[49] The notoriously long poem in the collection marks a crucial advance from the Surrealist and dreamy tone of his earlier late Modernist work. 'Europe' (and the emergence of his cut-out style) might be read, in this way, as Ashbery's thinking himself out of Modernism, part of which depends on his reworking of Modernist subject-matter. The poem is loosely set – if 'set' is the appropriate word – in England, and includes passages from *Beryl of the Biplane* (1917), an adolescent novel by William Le Queux about, as its subtitle suggests, 'the romance of an air-woman today'. The incorporation of this work of pulp fiction in a poem with such a lofty title is indicative of Ashbery's desire to articulate a new form of representation. It both shows how pulp might seductively be a 'menace to our way of life' and, playing on the idea of 'pulp', invests in the idea of cultural waste: references to 'dirt/ dirt you' are suggestive of the contexts in which forms of national identification take rise.[50] Although Ashbery would later come to feel that the poem was unsuccessful, 'Europe' proved hugely important and influential for his contemporaries: as Bill Berkson notes, reading it at the time, the poem 'had a surface like no other', with 'intervals' that were 'unique'.[51] Writing in a 1960 letter, O'Hara observes how it is 'so intriguing, compelling and attention-demanding, and mysterious' and referred to it as 'the most striking thing since *The Waste Land*'.[52]

The comparison is no coincidence (references to England, and its nineteenth-century legacies of European imperialism, abound) for Ashbery was self-consciously thinking about the possibilities of a fragmentary, montage-like poetics, freed of the mythological and expansive historical references of his Modernist forebearers that overdetermined the meaning of the poem (*Beryl* is repurposed rather than simply referenced). Writing 'Europe' was a way, as he later reflected in an interview with Koch, of 'at last permitting myself to allude to Europe, which had been my center of activity for several years'.[53] His technique to anchor the stream of impressions – 'merely listing a lot of things and situations that could be found in most other places as well and . . . keeping the ceramic title of the subway station firmly in mind' – was also a way to 'convey the impression that Europe was just another subject, no more important than a lot of others'.[54] In other words, in referencing Europe so explicitly in this poem, he was able to rethink what a major poetic work might be and how a new tradition might be formed. Ashbery wrote 'Europe' in 1958, at the height of the implementation of the Marshall Plan, which propelled the redevelopment that was underway in the city. It is hard to find any narrative in this work, let alone references to the poet's self, but there are occasional nods: markers of the poet's age – 33 – as we learn he is when writing 'Europe'. Ashbery himself describes the work as a way of starting over, as a kind of psychoanalytic experiment: 'just to clear my head by writing whatever came into it and that's very much the case in that poem'.[55] If the poem describes itself as written 'By an unseen hand', that invisible hand might also be considered the invisible hand of the market – of the emergence of new imperialist forms of a global financial order as we find in section 60:

> Wing
> > Bostonian
>
> and his comments
> thirty-three years old the day
> > of his third birthday the legs
> Lenin de Gaulle three days later
> > also comparing simple[56]

'Europe', a consciously post-war poem, implicitly confronts the horrors and the silences of Europe's recent history, a history that was perhaps made more intimate, for Ashbery, by Martory's own personal trajectory: he escaped Paris on the last train to leave the Gare d'Austerlitz before the Germans arrived and made his way to North Africa, where he joined the French Army, fighting alongside the Allied forces in Tunisia. For Ashbery, a collage-like poetics has the benefit of an 'inspiring asceticism of abstraction', as he writes of Joseph Cornell's work, that allows 'matter and manner [to] fuse to form a new element' so that 'we are allowed to keep all the stories that art seems to want to cut us off from.'[57] Collage allowed him to distance himself from the aesthetic landscape that he had created, an aestheticism that is, in part and paradoxically, the result of his taste for French language and culture. This new idea of asceticism – articulated most fully in 'The Ascetic Sensualists' (a poem which Ashbery later reflected that he sees 'no reason to have written or published') – is indicative of his desire to push his own writing to a new place through the collage unit.[58] The repurposing of found material parallels the work of the New Realists, and allows Ashbery to define his position through a double negative, an anti-non-identitarian position:

> I've always been anti anti-art. The fact is that it doesn't work, as Dada has proved – once you've destroyed art you've actually created it. It just has to be changed and chopped up a bit to take on a new beauty – like an Alexander McQueen frock.[59]

Ashbery here follows the New Realists' repudiation of critics' labelling of the movement, as expressed in Forty Degrees Above Dada, Pierre Restany's 1961 manifesto.[60] It is also a way of thinking of a project that might be more critical of Whitman's democratic poetic project a hundred years after its publication.

The title poem of the collection, 'The Tennis Court Oath', makes reference to an article in the *New York Times* on contemporary race relations. The poem is a sustained examination of how America's democratic ideals stand up a hundred years after its writing, an idea that is most powerfully evoked in the absence of a flag: 'No stars are there,/ No stripes,' as Ashbery writes in 'White Roses', a poetic analogy to Jasper Johns's white flags of America.[61] In a 1966 review of Johns's work, Ashbery remarks on 'his most astonishing productions in this present phase of history, when astonishment has become obsolete and practically inconceivable', producing work that has 'a new freedom and breadth' that allows for the rearranging of the debris of symbols into '"a completely new set of objects", in Wallace Stevens' words'.[62] Ashbery's style of art writing is continuous with the ways that his artistic friends spoke and thought of their work – outside of the rigours and formalism of Modernism, providing a natural counterpart to the works themselves. The personal responsiveness to the work, and the eschewal of the pretence to objectivity, escapes from the dual lens of the congratulatory and defamatory tone that defined the post-war spirit, thus evading the 'fist fights with the critic Clement Greenberg', which, as Ashbery notes, 'were almost de rigueur for New York artists in the fifties'.[63]

The intention of the New Realists centred on 'the direct appropriation of the real', which creates, as Ashbery writes, 'a common ground, a neutral language understood by everybody, and therefore the ideal material with which to create experiences which transcend the objects'.[64] In other words, writing about the 'New Realism' was a way of talking, indirectly, about the avant-garde. In his essay for the 'New Realists' exhibition catalogue, Ashbery locates in the artists' practice a way of accounting for 'the ambiguity of the artistic experience' by demonstrating how objects hold 'the balance of power . . . in the yet-once-again altered scheme of things'.[65] The essay, which seeks to situate the work historically, as a movement, rather than to describe any one work in detail, makes an unlikely reference to the insistently metaphorical language of T. S. Eliot, which saw a need to call 'the whole history of human thought into play'.[66] The desire to overcome the nature–art boundary, present in Ashbery's work since 'The Painter', is here brought to the forefront in the language of objects that 'makes it possible', as he notes, 'not to speak in metaphors'. The natural counterpart to the essay, 'The New Realism', is a poem that self-consciously explores what it means to speak without metaphor. The observations made in the essay are perhaps most interestingly explored in 'Idaho', the last poem in *The Tennis Court Oath*, which opens with an image of Jacques Tati-like clinical domesticity: 'He never failed to marvel at the cool, corrected elegance of the place as contrasted with its warm, rippling, honey-blonde occupant.'[67]

'Idaho', like all the poems in the collection, is a one-off experiment prompted by Ashbery's literary crisis that followed the publication of *Some Trees*, which resists assimilation into a dominative narrative. In this way, *The Tennis Court Oath* might be read not as individual poems, but rather as a book-length project – an experiment with what poetry might be. The poems take up images and repeat ideas so that America, seen through the lens of revolutionary France, becomes a way of thinking about the possibility of creating an alternative vision of what the nation might be. *The Tennis Court Oath* is not obviously a collection that is invested in the language of art, but it is a collection that is more visual than any other that Ashbery would write. It is also a collection that is intensely preoccupied by the inability to communicate: 'the coasts/ stammered with unintentional villages the/ horse strains fatigued I guess . . . the calls . . ./ I worry.'[68] The radical brevity of the lines and the incoherence of the statements prompt the reader to pause as they grapple with the impasse before them, articulated through the recalcitrance of language. The poems foreground the experience of living in the age of mass communication: newsprint saturates the collection, as Ashbery suggests that poetry's modes of communication cannot be isolated from the emergence of new mass-media forms.

Martory himself, as Ashbery notes, 'mistrusted America and her political institutions', and this atmosphere of mistrust makes itself felt in this much more self-consciously American collection, seen most clearly in its representative poems 'America' and 'Idaho'.[69] The idea of America is insistently explored through the prism of the legacies and the representational possibilities of

Revolutionary France. The title of the collection – *The Tennis Court Oath* – references the unfinished painting of the same name by Jacques-Louis David. The painting is the result of David's attempts to depict the political events of the French Revolution in 'real time', producing a new form of historical art, which has been judged by history 'to be less a way forward than a cul-de-sac for history painting'.[70] Ashbery himself recalls coming up with the idea in the Tuileries gardens on 'a beautiful day . . . watching young people in their tennis whites playing' and connecting this image with the image of 'the tennis court oath, which was such a serious violent event', noting that he subsequently discovered 'some wonderful David drawings for the painting; before he did paintings of clothed people he drew them naked'.[71] Ashbery was entranced by these sketches of 'naked men waving their hats in the air, one of which [he] tried to get Wesleyan [University Press] to use on the jacket, but they wouldn't'.[72] France provided the immediate setting for Ashbery to reflect on and engage with the French Revolution (and with the possibility of emancipation a decade before 1968 and the revolutions it would bring in its wake). Representing the French Revolution was also a way of thinking about the American Revolution that preceded it, and which set the stage for the revolutionary possibilities that would unfold in Europe in the last decades of the eighteenth century.

Throughout his career Ashbery eschewed any political identification (other than a broadly leftist position). But in spite of this ambiguity (or, as Ashbery would suggest, precisely because of it), his work insistently contests and destabilizes structures of power. His engagement with the difficulty and the provisionality of David's art, as well as his need to remake a historical genre, is also, by extension, a way of reflecting on the difficulty of representing a current or controversial political event – or indeed democracy (there are too many people in the painting that go unseen). The volatility of political circumstances forecloses the

Ashbery in Rome at the Villa Madama, 1963, photograph possibly by Fernando Sacco.

completion of the painting and opens up the need to rethink the terms of representation. In an interview with the Australian poet John Tranter, Ashbery suggests that the writing of *The Tennis Court Oath* – away from America – was, in part, made possible by the sense that 'if nobody's listening, then why not go ahead and talk to myself, and see what I get out of it.'[73] Ashbery found his isolation from the limelight of New York enormously liberating, reflecting that if he had been in New York, he might have felt the need to write for reviewers, but, in Paris, greatly enjoying the life in France, he was at least freed from the burden of writing to an audience. In the mysterious tone of 'How Long Will I Be Able To Inhabit the Divine Sepulcher', written at this remove from its immediate audience, Ashbery talks more explicitly to an imagined reader in the poem: a reader that would become all the more present and tangible on his return to New York in 1965, ushering in a poetics that was ready to assimilate the varied American idioms around it.

The final phase of Ashbery's Paris chapter saw the writing of his long poem 'The Skaters'. Begun around a year after 'The New Realists' exhibition in New York in Autumn 1962, it is a sustained meditation on the experience of living through a new kind of object-centred culture. Its long lines mark a shift away from the practice of fragmentation of *The Tennis Court Oath*, incorporating the principle of collage into its flow. The return to narrative (if an elusive version of it) after the disruptive strategies of *The Tennis Court Oath* opens up the possibility of a nonlinear associative logic that both anchors the reader while not relinquishing the ascetic possibilities that had been opened up by his recent work. As with 'Europe', the poem's European setting is at once everywhere and nowhere. There is one mention of Paris 1932, which is present, more suggestively, in the poem's inclusion of extracts from *Three Hundred Things a Bright Boy Can Do*, a 1910 book for children containing activities and craft projects that Ashbery found at a Paris *quai bouquiniste* (riverside booksellers). The book reminded him of the 1923 edition of the children's encyclopaedia *The Book of Knowledge*, which had been the centrepiece of his childhood imagination. As Ashbery told Bill Berkson in 1969, he had 'originally intended . . . to use the titles of the section(s) from that book as titles . . . I began this way, but then

Ashbery, *c.* 1964.

I found that the poem was a lot more mysterious if I removed the scaffolding of the titles.'[74] The composition process, however, was continuous with the recycling principle of *The Tennis Court Oath*: Ashbery lifts lines and phrases from his own unpublished work as well as from various other works, to create a new composite whole, one that finesses his principle of dis-identification in a poem that is also a sustained engagement not only with Wordsworth's *Prelude*, but with Thoreau's *Walden* (which also features skaters).

'The Skaters', which was written on a typewriter between Autumn 1963 and Spring 1964, and which first appeared in the Autumn 1964 issue of *Art and Literature*, was a farewell to the New York School poetics. The poem, which is divided into four parts, corresponding roughly with the four seasons of childhood, youth, maturity and age, is written in an obliquely autobiographical mode from the perspective of middle age. 'The Skaters' is, in many ways, a role reversal of 'Europe': Ashbery wanted to 'put everything in, rather than, as in "Europe," leaving things out'.[75] If the poem is a meditation on childhood, it is also one that demonstrates the aesthetic principle of selectivity – of what gets included in and left out – of a life and work. The long lines of 'The Skaters' work along a perspectival point that allows them to 'devour their own nature, leaving/ Nothing but a bitter impression of absence.'[76] The artist Trevor Winkfield reflected on hearing Ashbery read 'The Skaters' at the American Embassy in London in 1965, saying 'It was one of those life-changing events we often have in our receptive earlier twenties. I realized I could use poetry as an alternative sketchbook, a source of ideas.' Ashbery, he recalls, 'was dressed in a very "Ivy League" style – very clean cut with a tie', adding that 'every time he went to Harvard or Boston, he'd go to the conservative J Press men's clothiers store near Harvard Square': an 'expensive' spot![77]

'The Skaters', which is often read as Ashbery's version of the *Prelude*, is epic in scope, though its understanding of epic, and indeed of nature, is one that is grounded both in the banality of everyday rhythms as well as the logic of daydream: as Ashbery reminds us after a reverie, whatever his avant-garde ambitions, he is, nonetheless, writing this poem from a 'middle-class apartment'.[78] The long poem, informed by the work of French cultural theorists – and the publication of Barthes' *Writing Degree Zero* (1953), in particular – strives towards a kind of zero degree of autobiography: a place to start thinking about starting life afresh. The writing of the poem can be read in this sense, as Ashbery's way of acclimatizing himself to the prospect of returning to the USA. Paris, while initially an escape from the burdens of work, had become too conducive a place for work – and, inside his apartment, where poems about America were being written, the European landscape outside remained practically unchanged, a horizon that made the prospect of return to the States a little more palatable.

5

'The Invisible Avant-Garde': Turning Down Warhol, 1965–75

During his late Paris years, Ashbery returned to New York on
several occasions to give what were, for the local poetry scene,
legendary readings in 1963 and 1964. The poet Ron Padgett recalls
his shock at seeing and hearing for the first time the figure whose
work had already made such an impression on a group of younger
New York poets. At his reading at the Living Theatre in September
1963, Ashbery wore a silver-grey suit that Padgett described as
'hideous, with a metallic shimmer'. Ashbery took out a Gauloise
cigarette, and, as he was lighting it, looked up at the audience and
said, 'I get to smoke but *you don't*' and began to read. 'From having
read John's work,' Padgett recalls, 'I had expected an executive
voice, manly and strong and sure of itself. The words that came
out were in a nasal, almost whining voice.' But by the end of the
reading, though, 'his voice seemed perfect for those poems. I felt
they couldn't be spoken better in any other way.'[1]

Collaboration, conducted in various guises across the Atlantic,
continued to inform Ashbery's practice during these years; it was
the primary means through which he maintained his contact
with the New York School's aesthetic: writerly collaboration at
least, for, as Winkfield recalls, Ashbery 'hated collaborating with
painters!'[2] The Koch-Ashbery collaboration, 'New Year's Eve',
which Koch and Ashbery worked on in 1961, is characteristic of the
social dynamics and literary tone of these productions. Composing

the poem, Ashbery contributed the odd lines and Koch the even lines, each of which contains a place name and a drink, written in a contemporary take on Japanese linked verse. The poem was one of six Ashbery–Koch collaborations that were published in *Locus Solus* in 1961. Much like the Oulipo group who had recently formed in Paris, the collaborations make use of arbitrary constraints and 'amusing intricate rules' to compose a new kind of poetics. Often these collaborations feel forced by the rigidity of their constraints, but the spontaneity of 'New Year's Eve' suggests that it was written, first and foremost, to entertain. The poem, whose female protagonist, Anna, travels around the world, opens, in Surrealist fashion, with a vision of Europe transformed by new global forces: 'Water flowed slowly over the bridge in Danbury/ On New Year's Eve, while a Chicago of chocolate milk/ Formed in Zurich.'[3] Its fast-paced narrative follows in pursuit of Anna and all the assortment of products-as-characters she encounters along the way: '"Happy New Year!" thundered back the Ethiopian pineapple juice./ "Happy New Year!" screamed the Mexican hat./ "Good luck!" whispered the chocolate pear-juice.'

During the early 1960s Koch, Ashbery's foremost advocate, exercised his role as professor at Columbia University to 'indoctrinate' his students with John's work. One of the results of Koch's pedagogical enthusiasm was that one of his students (and a poet himself), David Shapiro, who would go on to write the first book on Ashbery, expressed to the publisher, Arthur Cohen, the importance of Ashbery's work. Soon afterward Cohen met Ashbery at an art opening and immediately told him he wanted to publish his next book. *The Tennis Court Oath* had been reviewed, for the most part sceptically, as the work of a poet who was entrapped in Modernism, but when Cohen published *Rivers and Mountains* (1966), 'the critics snapped back to him,' as Padgett recounts. 'It was a crucial turning point in the public reception of his work.'[4]

Rivers and Mountains, Ashbery's third collection, which was nominated for a National Book Award, marked a shift in his reception. The volume, which alludes to the self-conscious, if ironic, situation of his poetics within a landscape tradition, ushers in a new communicativeness, expansiveness and ambition in Ashbery's work. Its title poem opens with a secret map whose landscape proves hard to read as representation and reality are confounded: 'Your plan was to separate the enemy into two groups . . . But their camp had grown . . . To be the mountains and the map.' In a 1970 letter to Kenward Elmslie, Ashbery jokes about the date of the poem being later than supposed, casting a wry look at literary historical projects such as this one: 'In the case of "Rivers and Mountains" which I am always pointing out was written before Kennedy's assassination, on

Ashbery and Harry Mathews, Maison Pic Restaurant, Valence, France, October 1968.

account of the phrase about the "unassassinated president."' During his time in Europe, Ashbery stayed with Harry Mathews in Lans-en-Vercors in the French Alps, where *Art and Literature* was printed. The collection's meditation on an American landscape is accessed through the prism of a European one. Opening with the poem 'These Lacustrine Cities', it immediately presents the mountains of its title as a metaphor not so much of nature as the manmade monuments of our contemporary landscape – as Ashbery's own version of Elizabeth Bishop's 'The Monument'. Ashbery wrote the poem when 'thinking about a trip [he] made to Zurich'.[5] Zurich, he noted, was also near the place where the remains of the lake dwellers' 'civilization was discovered in the last century, and this might have had some bearing on my use of the word lacustrine'.[6] The discovery of the 'lake peoples', who built their settlements at different times from 43,000 to 800 BC, was a watershed for European archaeology, and this collection as a whole, written between Europe and the United States, meditates on the emergence of a new idea of historic time. 'What I think the poem seems to be about', Ashbery notes, 'is a kind of dream of history': history as a dream from which one is trying to awake was, of course, a common way of thinking in the immediate post-war moment.[7]

The facade of civilization in the wake of war (always apparent in Ashbery's interest in de Chirico's paintings) is explored most overtly in the collection in his pseudo-Freudian poem 'Civilization and Its Discontents'. Freud's essay of the same name, which meditates on the psychological cost of living in civilization, provides a counterpoint to Ashbery's sense of inertia in the image of a rapt crowd of spectators – 'A people chained to aurora/ I alone disarming you.'[8] It is in this at once expansive yet reticent collection that Ashbery begins to formulate the capacious use of the personal and multiple pronoun 'you' with which his work becomes synonymous. 'I prefer "you" in the plural, I want "you,"' he notes in 'A Blessing in Disguise', written in January 1962.[9] In

'Civilization and Its Discontents', he both aligns himself with that spectacle and positions the poem as promising its own vista of independence. The volume is suffused with death – with that of his father in particular, who passed away in 1964. In 'The Ecclesiast', we are offered a typically unsentimental image of death as something that is soberly inescapable and yet tinged with comic hyperbole: 'The monkish and the frivolous alike were to be trapped in/ death's capacious claw/ But listen while I tell you about the wallpaper.'[10] In 'Clepsydra', one of Ashbery's last poems written in Paris, he recalls 'feeling for the first time a strong unity in a particular poem . . . "Clepsydra" is really a meditation on how time feels as it is passing.'[11] Ashbery has said that his governing image of the poem was of a tall, narrow marble slab down which a single drop of water slowly trickles, but the poem, first published in *Art and Literature* in 1966, unfolds like a torrential river.[12] 'Clepsydra', which is in search of a subject, has as its quest the possibility of poetry in a moment of crisis, wrestling with the conundrum that 'A protected medium' was 'now giving itself the airs of a palace'.[13]

'Into the Dusk-Charged Air', which was written in 1961 and structured around Dada compositional procedures, is a poem unlike any other in the post-war American landscape. The poem is constructed as a 152-line catalogue of rivers that moves from the Danube to Ardèche, covering every river in between. It is, like 'Clepsydra', a hybrid poem that combines Ashbery's earlier experimental style with that of his inclusive middle-period. The discovery of Roussel's work and Oulipian constraints was important in fashioning this new style which, as Mathews notes in an interview with Ashbery, forces you 'to do things you wouldn't do otherwise'.[14] This catalogue of rivers comes close to the language of the manual, which produces in it, as Ashbery notes, 'effects of extraordinary limpidity' that feels transcendent while resisting a transcendental mode.[15] The result is a sense of the huge interconnectedness of the world at the turning point of a new period of internationalism. The poem opens with the Danube, which became a prominent interest to the Truman administration following the Second World War – the European Commission of the Danube has historically been seen as a unique organization that, through its success, continues to have implications for today's international order. The poem negotiates the use of the river as a metaphor for civilization in an epic poetic tradition and situates the post-war moment as a watershed epoch in which borders are redrawn and redefined. 'Into the Dusk-Charged Air' has the powerful flow of various rivers converging into an international source (thus shifting the 'river' poem from one that is grounded in an exploration of the idea of the nation). The word 'flow' takes on a prominence in the poem, creating a kind of recombined geography that suggests that any river may occur in any order, thus unsettling the whole enterprise of maps and territory-drawing that is central to the colonial imagination.

Ashbery's playful constraint is not, therefore, as it often is for the Oulipo group, merely an aesthetic device, but a principle for thinking through a new way of fitting the jigsaw puzzle of the global order together. The poem illuminates the ways in which an emergent global project also entails a flattening of previous models of internationalism that upheld imperialist projects. Imperialism is rarely considered a central subject of Ashbery's work, but the feeling of living through the 1960s, and the effects of America's cultural and political imperialism, suffuse his poems in these years.[16] The America that Ashbery found when he returned in 1965 was a country transformed by new technological and cultural developments: the Vietnam War was brewing, the space race was on the horizon and Civil Rights activists were marching for the Voting Rights Act. Ashbery returned to New York at the height of this volcanic shift in public formation, in mediated landscapes, in social protest and political organizing. There was a cultural revolution in Greenwich Village, which would be the centre of the Stonewall Riots of 1969, but Ashbery no longer lived there.

Ashbery with Jane Freilicher and Joe Hazan, photograph by John Gruen, *c.* 1960.

Back in the city, Ashbery resumed old friendships and made new ones. He moved into an apartment on East 95th Street on the Upper East Side, in the brownstone home of the painter Giorgio Cavallon, which, as he notes, was conveniently located for the subway.[17] This uptown residence was seen by an emergent younger generation of poets as denoting an upper-middle-class lifestyle that removed Ashbery from their more countercultural aims. Ashbery's own assimilation into the canon would be constantly on his mind during this period, a position which he formulates most clearly in his 1968 essay 'The Invisible Avant-Garde', which he wrote on a train to New Haven for a talk at Yale. In the essay, he positions himself as a part of an older generation recalling the moment when he found 'the avant-garde very exciting' – in 1950, to be exact – because 'there was no sure proof of the existence of the avant-garde,' which created the sense 'that one was poised on some outermost brink'.[18] The avant-garde's consequent assimilation into the tradition, an assimilation that parallels Ashbery's own trajectory, makes it necessary, he argues, to devise a new positionality 'which neither accepts nor rejects acceptance but is independent of it'.[19] Though Ashbery remained typically casual about the composition of this essay (dashed off on a train on the way to New Haven), it remained seminal to his thinking over the subsequent decades, in poems in which he demonstrates how the avant-garde comes full-circle on itself and contemplates the oddity that '*he*, not *it*, is [now] the avant-garde'. In the wake of artist celebrities, such as Pollock and Warhol, art, he saw, had taken a new turn. Ashbery reformulates this position in various guises in interviews, often declaring that his work gets all the attention at the same time that he suggests the importance of the cultivation of the artist as a figure of interest and of invisibility as the most powerful armour.

Back in the USA, Ashbery's poetry was once again interrupted by the demands of work. Newly employed at *ArtNews*, he recalls that 'it was sort of a hindrance to have to go to work every day, but

Ashbery and Gerard Malanga, New York, 1965–7.

on the other hand, Tom Hess was a very enlightened boss, though he could also be very tyrannical.'[20] Resuming the daily grind in New York, Ashbery found less time to write: 'I was really only writing poetry on weekends. I was a weekend poet.'[21] If his poetry had to take a backseat to the demands of work, however, Ashbery, nonetheless, remarked on how the scene had exploded since he had been away, recalling how his first poetry reading in the United States on his return from France at the Living Theatre 'was one of perhaps a dozen that were being held that night in various parts of the city'.[22] Whereas the poetry culture he had left was governed by a few 'elder statesmen', by the time he moved back in 1965 'there were readings everywhere, and the New York School of Poetry thing was an entity . . . the name itself had stuck.'[23] The establishment of the Poetry Project at St Mark's Church allowed an otherwise marginal poetry a means of dissemination by way of readings, lectures and performances, which became crucial to the democratization of poetry at mid-century and generated new communities of poets

Ashbery, New York, 1965–7.

that loosely became associated with the label 'Second Generation
New York School'. Ashbery attributes this 'poetry explosion in the
country' to the Beats 'and their habit of proclaiming their poems
in public places'.[24] Poetry Project reframed poetry's audience,
making its production and reception a much more culturally
integrative and dynamic affair. The Project had the effect of making
poetry, once seen as an outdated and staid genre, fashionable.
Andy Warhol and Lou Reed made an appearance, alongside poets
Gregory Corso, John Giorno, Joe Brainard and Bernadette Mayer: it
was a moment when the boundaries between poetry and other art
forms became more porous.

Warhol would prove a provocative figure for Ashbery. While
he claimed that Warhol never really interested him, Ashbery also
recalls writing 'a couple of appropriately "fascinated" articles on
him', the first of which acknowledges the seismic impact of Pop
Art, which caused 'the biggest transatlantic fuss since Oscar Wilde
brought culture to Buffalo in the nineties'.[25] Over and beyond

Warhol's revolutionary approach to mimesis, what seemed to interest Ashbery about Warhol was his attitude to fame, as well as his stance on taste. Warhol was 'both surprised and slightly bored by his success', a model that Ashbery would use in negotiating his own growing cultural status, and '[claimed] not to believe in art, although he collects paintings by fellow artists who have little in common with him, such as Joan Mitchell, Willem de Kooning and Fairfield Porter' – just the figurative styles that Ashbery, even in his more abstract moments, was drawn to.[26] Ashbery was also photographed by Warhol for his 1966 Screen Tests project, a cinematic form of photography that makes its subject fully aware that he is taking part in an artistic event. In his own prophetic version of the project, Ashbery's stubborn stare recalls the moment the shutter clicks in 'Little J. A. in a Prospect of Flowers'. In spite of Ashbery's ambivalence about Warhol's value, Warhol's work clearly spoke to him in a powerful and direct way. Shortly after his return from Paris, Ashbery attended Warhol's first Exploding

Andy Warhol, *Screen Test: John Ashbery* [ST13], 1966, 16mm film, black and white, silent, 4 minutes 6 seconds at 16 frames per second.

Plastic Inevitable event on St Mark's Place, at which the Velvet Underground played – an event that is cited as marking a definitive shift from New York's 1950s subculture to its 1960s manifestation, which artists Tony Scherman and David Dalton recall traumatized Ashbery: 'I don't understand this at all,' he reportedly said, before bursting into tears.[27] Ashbery's response, though often cited as reactionary, might be seen as indicative of a deep, emotional ambivalence about the changing cultural landscape.

The distinctions between the two generations of New York School poets were often framed by the younger generation, who sought to distance themselves from those they saw as their more traditional elders. Such a sentiment is captured in Tom Clark and Lewis Warsh's poem 'To John Ashbery': 'John/ it's/ cold out. You are going/ uptown,' which is to say, in the opposite direction to them.[28] The second generation sought to emphasize the upper-middle-class comforts that Ashbery's poetic production represented, while their own productions were staged as more provisional and collaborative. Downtown becomes a signifier of a more fugitive charm that is associated with the cold-water tenement apartments that lined the Lower East Side. If the Second Generation New York School would often frame their discrepancies with their forebears in terms of their proximity to the countercultural scene, Ashbery's work is, however, not as distanced from those changes as it might look at first sight – or is certainly not isolated from the sweeping countercultural wave that washed the American scene in the mid- to late 1960s. If Ashbery 'never had anything to do with rock and roll', he was, more broadly, interested in the emotional appeal of this cultural movement.[29] What it changed, for him in particular, was his sense of the reader: 'I always felt that the drug culture must have zeroed in on my poetry – at least I had visions of people sitting around and getting stoned, reading it aloud, and saying, "Man listen to this!"'[30] Ashbery is, in part, wryly commenting on his own remove from that scene while also suggesting a new desire to incorporate the porousness of that experience, one that comes to the fore in his subsequent collection, *Double Dream of Spring* (1970).

The waves of changes that were widely felt in 1966 were overshadowed by a more intimate sense of loss in the wake of O'Hara's death on 25 July 1966, at the age of forty, which had a seismic impact not only on Ashbery but on the New York cultural community as a whole. For Ashbery, the loss of O'Hara, who had 'cobbled' the scene together, and who had been a kind of twin to him in his early years, was hard to comprehend.[31] In his immediate eulogy for him, Ashbery registers O'Hara's death as monumental, having 'some of the incredibility and numbing after-effects of President Kennedy's'.[32] In the obituary he wrote for *ARTNews*, he manages to assimilate the absurdity of the event into something characteristic of O'Hara's work itself:

> It seemed, and seems, impossible that someone so involved with life, who in a sense reinvented it and translated it into a language which we could for once understand, could be abandoned by it. The fact that he was hit by a vehicle on Fire Island, where roads and traffic do not exist, added to our incredulity until we remembered that such violent anomalies are the stuff of Frank's poetry, and that they are rules, not exceptions.[33]

At O'Hara's burial service, held at Green River Cemetery in Springs, New York, Ashbery read O'Hara's poem 'To the Harbormaster'. Over the twenty years of their friendship, O'Hara wrote many poems dedicated to and about Ashbery, whom he affectionately referred to as 'Ashes'. Their intimate bond is recorded most evocatively in the vision of friendship in the afterlife that O'Hara imagines in his tender, heartfelt poem 'To John Ashbery', which opens,

I can't believe there's not
another world where we will sit
and read new poems to each other
high on a mountain in the wind.[34]

O'Hara's death marked the end of the heyday of the New York School:
with Schuyler living with the Porter family in Southampton and Koch
teaching at Columbia, the school suddenly took on a historical air.
For Ashbery, this transition meant the end of a 'remote period' of
youth which he looked back on as 'an almost idyllic one'.[35] Without
the 'radiant magnetism' of O'Hara, the sense of competition – as
well as community – that the New York School had furnished fell
away, leaving him to carry on writing in his uptown apartment. In
a later reflection on O'Hara, Ashbery notes the difficulty he had
'readjusting to New York and my new job at *ARTnews* after a decade
abroad, finding and furnishing an apartment, picking up the threads
of interrupted friendships, re-learning the New York *patois*'.[36] The
job had demanding after-hours duties: at the height of the season he
went to two or three events a night, sometimes only running into a
gallery for a few minutes – long enough to be seen. As Edmund White
recollects, 'Ashbery was always surrounded by art-world people,
which brought a whiff of money and internationalism to the usual
seedy gathering of poor poets. Like Warhol he gave the impression of
never trying.'[37] It was not all work – Rivers, Katz, Freilicher and Porter
were still around – but it was less of a coterie than when O'Hara
was still alive. This readjustment – and the emergence of a new
American *patois* – is written into the poems that Ashbery worked
on in the mid- to late 1960s, poems that incorporate comic-strip
characters and B-movie dialogue into their newly synthesized ascetic
aestheticism that make them 'pure products of America'.

The Double Dream of Spring, the collection that is written in
response to these movements, opens with a statement of fresh
concerns:

They are preparing to begin again
Problems, new pennant up the flagpole
In a predicated romance.[38]

Ashbery positions himself on the furthermost brink, from which
vantage point he stages the process of beginning again – the theme
that pervades this volume – in the wake of a series of deaths and
social upheavals that left him feeling unmoored. For the opening
poem, 'The Task', a poetic manifesto of sorts for this period, he
took his title from an eighteenth-century poem by William Cowper,
while the collection's title is taken from a 1915 painting by de Chirico,
on display at MOMA, in which a plan of a city and an interior is
outlined on an easel that stands in the foreground of a landscape.
In a 1966 review of de Chirico's *Hebdomeros*, Ashbery writes of the
'hypnotic quality' of the artist's work and his 'incredible prose style'
with 'long run-on sentences, stitched together with semicolons':

> In this fluid medium, trivial images or details can suddenly
> congeal and take on a greater specific gravity, much as a banal
> object in a de Chirico painting – a rubber glove or an artichoke
> – can rivet our attention merely through being present. His
> language, like his painting, is invisible: a transparent but dense
> medium containing objects that are more dense than reality.[39]

Something of this desire for a transparent style which
foregrounds the denseness of objects can be found in a number of
zany poems in this collection that are suffused with pop cultural
references. The zaniest, 'Farm Implements and Rutabagas',
which was published in the *Paris Review* in 1967 and opens 'The
first of the undecoded messages read: "Popeye sits in thunder,/
Unthought of"' marks a new transition to a more assimilative
poetic language.[40] Popeye appears in another Ashbery–Koch
collaboration, 'Death Paints a Picture' (1958):

The statue of Balenciaga was dripping onto other statues: among
those it dripped on was the statue of Popeye and the statue
of President Hoover, who was himself a statue, and the statue
of Swee'Pea, which lay at the foot of the statue of Popeye.[41]

In his papers, Ashbery kept an April 1967 copy of the Sunday
supplement of *El Diario*, the largest and oldest Spanish-language
newspaper in the United States, which contained a comic strip
of 'Popeye El Marino', a possible referent for the writing of 'Farm
Implements and Rutabagas'. In an interview with David Kermani
in 1974, Ashbery notes how 'Popeye's malapropisms . . . might
be another reason why I find him interesting, since I tend to
dislocate language myself.'[42] In the poem, Popeye is forced to
flee from his country, a position of exile, one that Ashbery might
have related to in his experience of self-exile to France. The ironic
use of the phrase '*For this is my country*' derives directly from the
Spanish-language comic strip, making it not only a meditation
on ideas of citizenship but an indirect reference to the waves of
Latin American migration that transformed New York districts
in the mid-1960s: those who were forced to live in a 'shoebox of an
apartment'.[43] Readers of 'Farm Implements and Rutabagas', as with
all the poems in the collection, find themselves stepping through a
looking glass into an alternative reality – a landscape of the mind,
only rather than the landscapes of Ashbery's earlier work, these
landscapes are often continuous with popular culture (Popeye
would also be a key figure for Warhol's mid-century work).

In 'Soonest Mended', Ashbery's iconic poem that meditates
on the process of continually re-beginning, the poet associates
himself with those 'Barely tolerated, living on the margin/ In
our technological society'. This is the position from which, he
suggests, we might imagine desired, difficult states, free from
the casual distraction that had become a daily hazard in a newly
mediatic landscape.[44] The drive of this difficulty, as Ashbery

expresses it, is 'to be small and clear and free'. The speakers in the poems – variously characterized as pilgrims, explorers and outsiders – have one common aim: to shake off the clutter of demands so that life is not simply an 'acting this out/ For someone else's benefit'. The complicated ambition that is articulated in the poem is how to reduce the daily variety of life to a manageable variant without being co-opted into a system – a question that would be at the forefront of Ashbery's next collection. Freedom, the poem suggests, can only be achieved through a breaking away, but one that avoids total secession by thinking on a minor scale, implementing slow divergences.[45]

Jane Freilicher, *John Ashbery*, 1968, oil on canvas.

'Fragment', a long poem written in fifty ten-line stanzas, the most sustained exploration of this theme, was written in 1964 and published as a book in 1969 with drawings by Alex Katz, who has described Ashbery's poems as 'fabulous', noting they have 'lots of visual images that just flash'. Ashbery sat for Katz three times: the first, in 1970, is a close-up in pencil of a sullen-looking Ashbery on the telephone, with a flicker of hair animating the image; a casual image also in pencil shows Ashbery on the sofa in his signature '70s style; and a side-angle portrait of the poet in 1986 adds Ashbery to Katz's signature cool portraits.[46] The poem, which Ashbery began writing at his parents' home when he returned for his father's funeral in 1964, and finished in Paris upon his return, opens with an impasse: 'The last block is closed in April.'[47] 'Fragment', which situates itself on the 'central perimeter/ Our imagination's orbit', establishes an errant motion that is characteristic of the continually wandering-away position of Ashbery's work that allows it to remain undefinable.[48] The fragment of the poem that makes itself whole fuses together as the poem ends, 'words like disjointed beaches/ Brown under the advancing signs of air'.[49]

Ashbery's own antipathy towards the protest poetry that emerged against the backdrop of the Vietnam War might be read as part of a desire to resist a systematic poetic language as opposed to a straightforward refusal of it; and he notes, accordingly, that though he did not enjoy partaking in anti-war poetry readings, 'the peace marches I went on seemed to me . . . *somewhat* more effective as a means of protest.'[50] Interestingly, at an anti-Vietnam War rally at Riverside Church in the early 1970s, rather than read his own poetry Ashbery recited Whitman's great Civil War poem 'The Wound-Dresser'. L. S. Asekoff recalls how Ashbery's voice trembled as he read it and at some point his voice cracked, he began to sob and was unable to finish reading.[51] There are no obvious Ashbery war poems, but his 1972 book of prose poems *Three Poems* builds towards an anti-systematic language that resists co-optation. Ashbery describes the project as 'a kind of discourse that's almost like a landscape that one can get lost in and explore and find new things all the time'.[52] In *Three Poems* he turns to the 'ugliness' of prose as a novel solution to a style that he found had crystallized a little too easily in *The Double Dream of Spring*. The long, continuous flow of the poems creates the effect of a system breaking down – a familiar feeling in the early 1970s – coupled with a drive to renewal. Its second poem, 'The System', articulates an idea of renovation that incorporates, without hierarchy or framing quotation marks, language assimilated from public spheres as a kind of deflationary rhetoric. This shifting of the ground of the poetic to the public, staged through the prose poem (a form that is distinctly un-American), aims for a reproduction of a crisis that was unfolding around the country, with a faith in poetry's ability to at least articulate that terrible scene, if not intervene in it.

Ashbery, who imagined *Three Poems* as 'three oblong empty boxes to be filled with anything', discussed its composition with his Chilean psychoanalyst, who recommended that he write 'about all the people who've meant most to you in your life, and then don't write about them, but write about what you think when you think about them'.[53] Ashbery worked furiously, composing as fast as he could type (which was fairly fast). In a 1972 review of Ashbery's work, Richard Howard gives one of the most astute assessments of *The Double Dream of Spring* – and indeed of Ashbery's work as a whole – noting how

> the poems were moving toward – and some had already
> moved right in on – *prose*, an utterance unpoliced (the policy
> turning out to be 'to keep asking it the same question/
> Until the repeated question and the same silence become
> answer'), innovative or advanced, as everyone keeps saying
> about this writer, because the lines were not wielded to

Ashbery on the beach with Jane Freilicher, 1967.

convey the disciplinary, punitive passion which has always been the art's contribution and conventional resource.[54]

The early 1970s continued to be busy time for Ashbery, who was immersed in the art world. In a 1970 letter to Elmslie, he recounts a typical summer, spent jetting around the Hamptons with his then lover the New York art dealer Aladar Marberger, with whom he is 'mostly together . . . except for inevitable separations such as going to my analyst'. It was, he writes, 'one of those dank, chilly Hamptons weekends we all know so well. There was an art party that was very heavy with gossip and bitchery, which caused Jane to remark, "It's all starting very early this year – this seems like Labor day weekend."' A little later, Ashbery writes to Elmslie:

> I'd love to come by and 'visit' you. Could this be the first week in August? I have to be at Swohegan for a 'gig' on the 9th and would like to spend a few days with those luscious fruits in sweet cahoots who are the administrative staff, returning via the Katzes to New York and thence to Pultneyville. I then plan to work the last two weeks in August and take September off, perhaps to visit San Francisco. Wouldn't you like to come? Now that I've found I don't mind flying so much I'm eager (perhaps anxious would be a better word) to try it again.[55]

After five years apart from Martory, Ashbery had once again settled down into a comfortable domestic arrangement, with David Kermani, who would be his partner until his death in 2017. Soon after meeting in 1970, Kermani, who was nineteen years Ashbery's junior, began working on a comprehensive bibliography of Ashbery's work, and eventually began managing his business affairs. Not only a lifelong partner, Kermani was also Ashbery's most dedicated reader: he decided to publish Ashbery's art reviews, believing that, although Ashbery refused to explain his poems, if readers were able to make the same connections that he did, they would understand the poetry better. In an effort to ensure that his bibliography conformed to scholarly protocols, he undertook a Master's degree in library science at Columbia in 1976.

Though Ashbery and Kermani were together for 42 years, their personal relationship was, especially in the 1970s, fairly open (Kermani was engaged to a couple of women over the years).[56] The post-Stonewall years, for Ashbery, ushered in a new period, if not of newfound queer liberation, at least of queer ease. A 1970 letter to Schuyler opens, accordingly, in full camp mode: 'Dear Gay Pride of Pride's Crossing', referring to 'Gay Pride' week 'in Manahatta', a term, he notes, which 'seems both curiously redundant and strangely apt to me', taking a cautious distance from 'the new militants', by playfully referring to it as 'a nice name for a new brand of whipped-cream mayonnaise'.[57] It was in the late 1960s

David Kermani and Ashbery, summer 1977, photograph by Clarice Rivers.

and early 1970s that Ashbery first cultivated his reputation as a fine cook and dinner-party host, one that remains a touchpoint with his former French life ('pps', he writes in another letter to Schuyler, '"Cassoulet toulousain" now seems like a terrible blemish, and I've discovered that they do in fact say "gratin dauphinois"!!!!!').[58]

Douglas Crase recollects seeing Ashbery for the first time in 1972, 'slouched in the doorway of the dining room' at a dinner party he had crashed at the Rochester Oratorio Society:

> He was, to get this on record, sexy. He seemed intent on it and he looked as he does in the now-famous photograph taken a year earlier by Gerard Malanga on Eighth Street-full mustache, unruly hair, and a practiced slouch that was part boredom and part come-hither-if-you-dare.[59]

Ashbery and James Schuyler in front of Jane Freilicher paintings, in Walter Mill, New York, c. 1968.

Ashbery and Douglas Crase, Niagara Falls, 1975.

The image was taken after a brief encounter between poet and poet-photographer in Greenwich Village one spring day in 1971 after an April shower. Malanga recalls Ashbery sending him a letter forty years later in return for the print: 'Thanks so much for the wonderful print! (Was I ever really that thin?) It was most generous of you. Fondly, John Ashbery'.[60] Crase would assume the role of chauffeur when Ashbery visited his mother in upstate New York (Ashbery only learnt to drive in 1971, practising at his mother's house in Pultneyville). 'If these were pleasure trips for him they counted as field trips for me,' he notes, 'made instructive by the exemplary way he indulged his interests and wasn't ashamed of them. He could spend hours looking through old postcards at the used book store in Springwater, a favorite.'[61]

In 1972 *ArtNews* was sold and Ashbery was fired, leaving him out of work for a year. The early 1970s were, nonetheless, for Ashbery a time marked by increasing international recognition and the travel it brought with it: he only began to take planes regularly in 1971, which opened up new opportunities to accept invitations abroad. Ashbery's style, as much as his poetics, embraced the 1970s: like a figure out of a Robert Altman film, he wore his hair long, sported a full moustache, a loose shirt and an adopted, casual assuredness about his role as an artist that reflected his growing recognition. A fur-trimmed leather jacket also became a staple of these years, completing what he referred to as his 'Mexican Bandit Look'.[62]

The poet's zip code had, too, become more fashionable: Ashbery spent the 1970s in Chelsea before taking up residence in the colonial revival house in Hudson, upstate New York, that he bought in 1978. He had moved into a tall post-war building on the edge of the Chelsea neighbourhood, on West 25th Street, moving four years later, in 1974, to a unit on a higher floor, located in the rear. Space was important to Ashbery and he finally found the arrangements he was looking for in Chelsea. The apartment's bland, anonymous quality, like the one he would later move into in 1984, combined with its cultivated disorder, made it an undetermined, freeing place to be, where he could imagine his own environment. Kermani, who lived with Ashbery for many years in Chelsea and Hudson, describes Ashbery's domestic arrangements in terms that might equally serve as a description of his style:

> Living with John is very difficult. Everything needs to be open and nothing is ever closed. Drawers. Cabinets. Closet doors. Everything! All possibilities must be available at all times, and there's no order to it – it's not this stack is for this and that stack is for that.[63]

Ashbery describes Chelsea as 'an alternative to Greenwich Village as that became more and more expensive' before the district too became 'discovered'.[64] His apartment, which was flooded with the sound of the city street below, looked out towards the Hudson River and the heights of New Jersey – much as in a Freilicher painting. The New York cultural scene was still relatively small in the 1970s when 'it was [still] easy to meet John Ashbery or Jasper Johns,' as Frank O'Hara's biographer Brad Gooch recollects.[65] According to the social commentator Fran Lebowitz, everyone who read Andy Warhol's *Interview* knew one another – this included Ashbery – and this small world located downtown had a lasting influence on American taste in the arts. Ashbery is included in Edmund White's survey of the 1970s cultural scene as one of New York's representative figures and cultural arbiters, alongside Sontag, Johns, George Balanchine, Robert Wilson, Robert Mapplethorpe and Richard Sennett. A 1975 portrait of Ashbery by Peter Hujar, one of the key figures in New York's downtown art scene, confirms his presence among this iconic set of artists and intellectuals.

Joe Brainard was one of the new generation of New York artists and poets who would become a central presence in Ashbery's life in the 1970s. Ashbery described Brainard's work in a 1977 interview

Ashbery's Chelsea apartment, 2008.

as 'very straightforward and succinct, yet subversive in this straightforwardness and succinctness'. Ashbery wrote *The Vermont Notebook* in 1974 and sent the work to Brainard, who illustrated the text, which was published by Black Sparrow Press the following year.[66] The book is set up so that every left-hand side features a black-and-white drawing by Brainard and each right-hand side features a poem by Ashbery. Ashbery opens a June 1974 postcard to Brainard:

Just got a letter from John Martin asking about the illustrations. Would you write to him? I was going to enclose the letter but seem to have lost it in this swamp of an apartment. Harry and I once visited the town [Lacaune-les-Bains] where this fountain is just to see it. How are you? New York is a summer Factory. All the really worthwhile people have gone away.

A year later he writes: 'Dear Joe, David and I are in San Francisco, enjoying the sights. (We are at the Mark Twain, a gay hotel) & had a nice time visiting Brainard Lake in Colorado – it looks like it was drawn by you'.[67]

The Vermont Notebook is a play on the idea of waste: there are riffs on and nods to Stein's *Tender Buttons*, Eliot's 'The Waste Land', Stevens's 'Man on the Dump', Duchamp's readymades and Warhol's Pop Art, making it a kind of curiosity cabinet of the American pastoral and the American vernacular. These poems, typeset at the bottom of the page, start off laconic and build towards a sequence of idiosyncratic lists: variously, of American poets, artists, cities, newspapers, paraphernalia and forms of violence. Packed full of rural and urban objects, the work is a meditation on the various forms of American dumps, an idea that circles back on itself: 'The dump escapes the true scape of the telling and in so doing is its own scape – the dump dumped and dumping.'[68] Ashbery wrote the poems while on a bus, which, he notes, was 'not the most poetic place', but the activity was 'an experiment in writing in an uninspiring environment', partly in Vermont, on the way to Kenward Elmslie's house, where Ashbery and Elmslie would spend the summer together, and parts of the book were published in Elmslie's *ZZ Magazine*. In a July 1974 letter to Elmslie, Ashbery writes that he's 'been writing quite a lot of poetry' but fears he has 'overextended' himself:

> it has come out very scratchy and peculiar. Last weekend David and I flew up to Pultneyville . . . and were lavishly entertained by Doug and Tom. And tomorrow I'm due to go out and spend a day with Kenneth so he can tell me how to teach. Thence to the Dash dacha for the weekend. After that . . . well, I am sort of thinking of Europe, but it would sure be nice to spend a few days with you and Joe and Auntie W.

The collaborative process is left purposefully ambiguous. As Ashbery explains, Brainard 'did the illustrations after I wrote it. Sometimes it has something to do with the text on the following page and sometimes it has nothing to do with it, and sometimes it could or couldn't have something to do with it.'[69]

The collaboration evidences a new materiality of language in Ashbery's work in the period, as can be seen in his beautiful poem 'A Man of Words', published in *Poetry* in November 1973, where print itself seems to leave the page, alerting the reader to the experience of reading: 'not the metallic taste/ In my mouth as I look away, density black as gunpowder . . . like the pressure/ Of fingers on a book suddenly snapped shut.'[70] Though in many ways overshadowed by the publication of *Self-Portrait in a Convex Mirror*, *The Vermont Notebook*, which Ashbery likens to his other collaborations, *Fragment* and *Turandot and Other Poems*, is an important work in its own right, particularly in its suggestiveness of the role of desire – heterosexual and homosexual – in upholding

Ashbery and Joe Brainard, Vermont, *c.* 1971/2.

American values in the mid-1970s. 'Dump' is understood politically,
not only as the bodies that are cast off as undesirable, but as
the earth's own inability to cope with the excesses of capitalist
production. *The Vermont Notebook* contains Ashbery's most overtly
scathing critique of the interests of big business, here wearing an
ostensibly green guise:

> While finding ways to protect and enhance the environment
> for an endangered species like the bald eagle is making big
> news these days, it should be only a preview of what we might
> expect from the $750,000 ecology program being funded by the
> Miami-based Deltona Corporation, developers of Marco Island.[71]

An April 1975 *Newsweek* article titled 'The Cooling World', which featured on a series of late-night TV shows, followed by a scientific paper in August that foresaw a period of pronounced global warming, set the tone for one of the first heated public debates in the United States about climate change. The book concludes with three letters or postcard messages, recycled from one of Ashbery's earlier unpublished poems, 'American Notes', demonstrating the found material and continual reuse principle applied to Ashbery's own work as a kind of self-consuming poetic machine.

The Vermont Notebook is a publication that resolutely refuses the idea of nature as some transcendental ideal that precedes the cultural, offering a reading that instead locates nature within culture in the trope of the dump. In one section that opens 'Dear Autumn Addict', Ashbery invents a character called Oscar, who 'resembles a portrait by [the nineteenth-century French painter] Carolus Duran': the book gave Ashbery scope to experiment somewhere between a lyric and a narrative voice in puzzle pieces that build towards a surreal portrait of the Vermont landscape – as representative of America as a whole.

In *Self-Portrait in a Convex Mirror*, the major work that he would write that year, it is hinted that the locus of crisis is New York in the mid-1970s, which was experienced as a pressure-cooker environment as it underwent a transition to a post-Fordist economy. 'The broken buildings and rubbled lots on the ground were both inspiration', as Andrew Strombeck notes, 'of the crisis's dominant narrative – that the city's welfare state had failed – and a product of its constrained vision of the city's life. As landlords walked away from more and more buildings, New York began to seem a wild place where anything could happen.'[72] Near the opening of *Self-Portrait in a Convex Mirror*, we read, accordingly, of the climate in which the poem is produced, in a world that was experiencing the first effects of globalization, where everything becomes a little more difficult to discern:

The shadow of the city injects its own
Urgency:
                    . . . New York
Where I am now, which is a logarithm
Of other cities. Our landscape
Is alive with filiations, shuttlings;
Business is carried on by look, gesture,
Hearsay.[73]

6

'I'm Famous for Being Famous': The Decade of Self-Inventiveness, 1975–84

Self-Portrait in a Convex Mirror, which won the Pulitzer Prize for Poetry, the National Book Critics Circle and the National Book Award, catapulted Ashbery to a fame that neither he nor the poetry world could have imagined. As Edmund White recollects, referring to its eponymous title poem,

> With this one poem Ashbery, intimate but impersonal, pinpointed the shifting uncertainty of the way we live now . . . It was as if we were seeing Whitman on Staten Island ferry or Emily Dickinson wrapping a cake and scribbling a poem on the paper.[1]

The work, which has been viewed as Ashbery's masterpiece, takes on a new argumentative style, one that becomes symbolic of a post-war self-defensiveness and 1970s paranoia in an era of new forms of surveillance and mediatized modes of representation. The convex mirror of the title poem takes as its referent and interlocutor the Italian Renaissance painter Parmigianino's 1524 painting *Self-Portrait in a Convex Mirror*.

Ashbery had first been drawn to the work when he saw it in a *New York Times* book review in 1950, and he later viewed it in the flesh in Vienna, in 1959, during his European stay. The writing of the poem was prompted by his coming across an inexpensive portfolio of Parmigianino's work, with the self-portrait illustrating the cover, displayed in the window of a bookstore in Provincetown in February 1973, during a month-long residence at the Fine Arts Work Center. The significance of the bookstore reinforced his 'half-conscious wish' to write about the painting. But, as in a Freudian dream narrative, the bookstore is made, in Ashbery's telling, a convenient fiction – a fable of the mysteries of artistic creation: it 'just materialised for a few moments to allow me to buy this book, and then vanished'. When he tried to find it again, 'it was like De Quincey looking in vain for the store where he first bought opium.'[2]

'Self-Portrait in a Convex Mirror' is a psychological poem that revolves around the difficulty of analysing the present – 'Tomorrow is easy, but today is uncharted' – to the extent that one lives by projecting dreams about the future, and these projections remove us from an immediate engagement with the present.[3] Ashbery is also saying something about language: that it is 'only speculation/ (From the Latin speculum, mirror)'. In other words, language mediates our environment – it is like a radio transmitter – 'No words to say what it really is, that it is not/ Superficial but a visible core.'[4] The poem emerged over a long gestation period of several months and 'required seemingly endless revisions'.[5] This new revisionary streak, which characterizes the collection as a whole, was something new for Ashbery, and indicative of the conceptual nature of his writing during this period. The poem takes on the essayistic tone of a mock art-historical essay but, as Ashbery concedes in an interview, 'the Parmigianino painting . . . is a pretext for a lot of reflections and asides that are as tenuously connected to the core as they are in many of my poems which, as you know, tend to spread out from a core idea.'[6]

The convex model of self-portraiture offered Ashbery, more explicitly, a metaphor for his coy, evasive relation to his own work: the painter's 'right hand/ Bigger than the head, thrust at the viewer/

And swerving easily away, as though to protect/ What it advertises.' The poem, rather than drawing upon life material, becomes a medium for reflecting on the relation between life and art.[7] The 1984 Arion Press edition of *Self-Portrait in a Convex Mirror*, made in an edition of 150 to mark the poem's ten-year anniversary, and which features prints by Richard Avedon, Alex Katz and Elaine and Willem de Kooning, is testament to the pivotal cultural and social transition that Ashbery symbolically frames as a 'life englobed':

> This otherness, this
> 'Not-being-us' is all there is to look at
> In the mirror, though no one can say
> How it came to be this way. A ship
> Flying unknown colors has entered the harbor.[8]

'Why can't you write poetry like that?', the ever-plainspoken, New York-based writer Mary McCarthy posed in response to a review by Ashbery in *Tribune*: the implication being that his prose was much more lucid than his poems.[9] Ashbery concedes that fifteen years of writing art reviews 'created this feeling of trust in readers and suspicion in myself'.[10] The practice of writing reviews, and Kermani's sense that Ashbery's art writing offers itself as a language to explain his work (thus doing away with the need for criticism) might well lie behind this move towards a more essayistic form.

For Ashbery, the poem is also about the idea of the artist figure – or indeed anyone who gets to be the centre of attention – making it, by extension, a reflection on how new technological forms of communication were altering both the machinations of power and the idea of the self as a unified thing. Surprised by the success of the poem, Ashbery remarked mock-coyly in an interview, 'I was a bit jealous that the book got the attention that I thought belonged to me.'[11] This playful version of Warhol's figuration of the artist is, for Ashbery, also a way of reinventing poetry's relationship to its audiences at a time when the culture of celebrity was changing the cultural landscape, one that was dominated by the cult of personality. As Wayne Koestenbaum notes: 'he merely needed to stand next to them . . . his Andyness could *sign* the adjacent presence, make it Andyish.'[12] Ashbery's own version of the cult of fame was typically more ironic, as he suggests in a 1985 interview with John Ash: 'I'm a superstar, almost like Edna Everage!', wryly noting that 'the jury is still out on the question of whether I'm a poet at all, yet I get my picture taken for *Women's Wear Daily*.'[13]

Ashbery had become a much more photographed presence in the mid- to late 1970s, and the title of 'Self-Portrait', which articulates itself in terms of a problem of posture and imposture, foregrounds a vocabulary of disguise and exposure that might be read in the light of the contemporary political mood. In 1974 America was embroiled in the Watergate scandal, the discovery, investigation and aftermath – the impeachment of President Richard Nixon – of bugging devices and photographic equipment used by the president's administration against the Democratic Party during the 1972 presidential election. *Self-Portrait* was written in a climate of secrecy and distrust that arose from new forms of surveillance and security testing. The title poem, which was first published in the August 1974 issue of *Poetry*, the same month that Nixon resigned from office, situates itself in a 'veiled, compromised' situation.[14] A new sense of impasse is registered in these poems in which 'All things seem mention of themselves,' as Ashbery writes in 'Grand Galop', and the poet is forced to reflect on his role: 'To try to write poetry/ Using what Wyatt and Surrey left around'.[15] Leisure is an idea that Ashbery's mid-period work returns to constantly, as, in part, an avant-garde poet's own reckoning with his middle-class positionality. In *Three Poems* he writes of contemporary experience as 'what distractions for the imagination, incitements to the copyist, yet nobody has the leisure to examine it closely'.[16] But he, nonetheless, assumes the role of the poet who examines the leisure time that is needed for 'the average, open-minded, intelligent person who has never interested himself before in these matters', as he writes in 'The System', either from not having had the leisure to do so or from ignorance of their existence.[17]

In 1974 Ashbery took up the role of professor of English at Brooklyn College, where he conducted an introduction to poetry, an undergraduate writing seminar and a postgraduate writing workshop, in addition to supervising individual tutorials. In a letter to Elmslie in September 1974 he recounts that his 'days have become a trice more hectic since I began to teach, if that's what it is I am doing. I really feel very uneasy and depressed about it.' Although his attitude to teaching remained ambivalent, he conceded that a couple of poems in his next collection, *Houseboat Days* (1977) – 'What is Poetry' and 'And *Ut pictura poesis* Is Her Name' – emerged from the process of beginning to teach poetry to students for the first time, during a period when literary theory was starting to make its presence felt in the American academy. As he reflects in an interview:

> Right after I began teaching, when I was in my late forties, I wasn't used to students asking me 'Why is this a poem?' or 'Why isn't this a poem?' or 'What are poems?' I never really thought about it – I'd just been writing poems all these years. So, from thinking about the nature of poetry came this admittedly slight and light partial answer to the question, 'What is Poetry?'[18]

The poem ends with a meditation on the uncertain role of poetry: 'It might give us – what? – some flowers soon?'[19] The difficulty with 'The Explanation', as he suggests in his poem of that title, is that 'Nothing' about the composition or the environment of the poem 'is too "unimportant"/ Or too important, for that matter. The newspaper and the garbage/ Wrapped in it, the over, the under.'[20]

Teaching was, nonetheless, a job – the kind of labour that Ashbery had been anxious to avoid since his days in publishing, and he did not take to the less creative parts of his teaching duties too willingly. As one of his students recollects, 'John appeared if not overwhelmed at least burdened and bewildered by the sheaf of documents in his arms: department directives, student registration forms (to be filled out in triplicate), class roll books, etc.'[21] Teaching was stressful for Ashbery, and he was also reluctant to travel out to Brooklyn, comfortable as he was in his Chelsea apartment. As the activist Al Sharpton notes, if things were considered bad in the 1970s and early 1980s in New York, 'things were 50 times as bad in Brooklyn as they were in Manhattan'.[22] Nonetheless, good living was still relatively cheap: Winkfield recalls that 'in the 1970s, John, Kenward Elmslie, Joe Brainard, Jimmy Schuyler and I were in the habit of having dinner at Duffs on Christopher Street – a three course meal could be had for around $15 (!).'[23]

The mid-1970s was a period when Ashbery found himself adjusting to the attention that went with his new prominence in the literary landscape. It was a period when the interview became the dominant form by which critics sought to understand contemporary poetry – which was met with reluctance from Ashbery, who eschewed any easy explanation of his work. A 1976 *New York Times* interview introduces his work as 'extremely difficult, if not often impenetrable'.[24] The difficulty, as emerges in conversation with Richard Kostelanetz, is less about a desire for difficulty in and of itself than a refusal to lock anything into place, which, as he writes in 'Self-Portrait', is 'death itself'.[25] Contrarily, interruptions – people – are life itself. The work in *Self-Portrait in a Convex Mirror* is structured around constant visitations from a flow of visitors, interruptions that are both testament to the sociality of the 1970s for Ashbery and his poems' long gestation. Interruptions are central to Ashbery's technique. As he notes, 'When I'm working, I don't mind answering the phone, since often my train of thought will be interrupted for the better. John Cage taught me that whatever interruption happens is part of the piece of music.'[26]

The poems become, accordingly, more conversational: breaking into dialogue, they make the moment of communication a live act. The mirror of the collection's title does not, however, reflect the poet's self but rather his otherness: 'this "Not-being-us" is all there is to look at/ In the mirror.'[27] Admitting this otherness is a way of imagining a concept of identity that is not blindsided by its own identifications. It is also an admission of the complexity of communication: we love to express ourselves and yet hate the idea of being forced to – an idea that Ashbery experienced acutely at this moment, pressed as he was to provide a critical vocabulary for his own poems.

This complexity is also apparent in the discursive and stylistic variation of his next and best-loved collection, *Houseboat Days*, which demonstrates a much more deliberate, and communicative, attempt to capture the spirit of America in the mid-1970s. 'Daffy Duck in Hollywood', which is set in Los Angeles, is illustrative of the poet's newfound loquaciousness, drawing upon the tension in everyday expression and the world of animation, which becomes a driving concern of Ashbery's work during this moment. 'The storm finished brewing', which comes mid-way through the rollicking poem, is a line that Ashbery would later chuckle over.[28] One of Ashbery's idiosyncratic talents is the ability to fuse a whole different register of references from opera scenarios to pop songs and advertising jingles, to combine passages from medieval and Renaissance texts with contemporary American life and, by the late 1970s, this technique becomes its own entirely inimitable language (no matter how younger generations will try to reproduce it).

Ashbery has described Daffy Duck's predicament as resembling that of Satan in *Paradise Lost*.[29] He was referring, in particular, to the Daffy Duck cartoon *Duck Amuck*, 'in which you see the artist's pen being dipped in the inkwell and then drawing Daffy, and then sort of tormenting him by adding an extra beak or drawing a monster about to destroy him', yet 'all the time the artist is invisible.'[30] It is typical of Ashbery's work that he uses the most comical of forms to get at the invisible hand of violence. Rather than describe it, the poem reproduces a mediatic, technological landscape where 'everything is getting choked to the point of/ Silence.'[31] The poem reflects on its own use of language: how 'its/ Grammar, though tortured, offers pavilions/ At each new parting of the ways.'[32] The genre of animated cartoons serves, in this way, as a historically specific mode of screen representation in Ashbery's work, in which an overly stylized, hard-boiled language foregrounds the ambiguous state of human agency in the post-Fordist era.

Explaining the choice of title for *Houseboat Days* in an interview, Ashbery notes that he lifted it from an issue of *National Geographic*, whose cover reads, 'Days in Old Kasmir': 'I sort of liked the kind of homely, old-fashioned sound of the phrase "Houseboat Days" . . . the idea of both . . . being on the move and being stationary in one's home – which is sort of what life is like.'[33] He might also have had in mind the lines from Elizabeth Bishop's 'Crusoe in England': 'Home-made, home-made! But aren't we all?'[34] Ashbery, who met his much-admired fellow poet in 1976, was, in fact, responsible for the epigraph used in her last book *Geography III* (1976). Bored and visiting his mother in the mid-1970s (he would spend a couple of weeks there every summer), he found a little textbook that had belonged to a student at a school in Sodus in the 1880s and sent it to Bishop, who included a couple of the lessons at the front of the book (much like Ashbery's use of textbooks in 'The Skaters'). Ashbery and Bishop locate in each other's work a sense of paradox that constantly evades interpretation, and which bears continual rereading. Puzzling over the sense of 'motion' that is created in *Three Poems*, Bishop writes to Ashbery in March 1973, of how he has 'arrived at a personal, purely logical, and deep – as well as beautiful way of saying things' and declares the book 'very important'.[35] The sentiment is echoed in his 1969 review of her *Complete Poems*: 'From the moment Miss Bishop appeared on the scene, it was apparent that she was a poet of strange, even mysterious, but undeniable and great gifts.'[36]

The poems in *Houseboat Days* contemplate the paradoxical position articulated in its title: the idea of opting for a provisional model of domesticity. It is also crucially a volume that meditates on the idea of Americanness through an off-centred perspective. In 'Pyrography', the centrepiece of the collection, we hear the voice of America itself, on an airwave that the poem picks up: 'This is America calling:/ The mirroring of state to state/ Of voice to voice on the wires.'[37] The poem, which sets itself up as a 'revolving stage set in Warren, Ohio', creates a sense of intimate knowledge – a secret thing that is known by 'those at the turn of the century' as the 'it' that constitutes American identity.[38] Far from Whitman's proclamative ideals, here Ashbery neither mythologizes a historical origin of the synecdochal nor suggests a final utopian ideal, but rather finds a perspective from which he is 'able to write the history of our time', which, he suggests, depends on turning partially away from its major events and figures: 'not just the major events but the whole incredible/ Mass of everything happening simultaneously and pairing off,/ Channelling itself into history'.[39]

'Pyrography' was written as a commission for the Department of the Interior, which had assembled an exhibition of paintings of American landscapes, 'America 1976', that travelled around the country as part of the bicentennial celebrations. After initially feeling that he could not write to commission, once Ashbery learned how much they would pay him, he decided it would not be so difficult after all. The challenge gave Ashbery's work a new communicativeness; his insights into the stage set of America depend on the distance he takes from his own enterprise. In photographs that Larry Rivers took for his accompanying 1977 artwork, we see Ashbery in a variety of different Ashberyean poses

– set against an Americana backdrop, camply reading a magazine, bored, seductive, on the telephone, inside, accompanied by Kermani – until Rivers chose the image he would work from: of the poet looking at the camera in the midst of typing his poem.

The two-part cover of *Houseboat Days* is split between a black-grey strip and a black-and-white painting of a woman on a boat by R. B. Kitaj. In a 1979 review of Kitaj's work, Ashbery explains that 'what is precisely new and exciting in Kitaj's work is the immense culture which saturates it but seldom appears there frontally. The works teem with references to films, poetry, novels and photography, but they make their effect with purely plastic means.'[40] As ever, it is an apt description for the discursiveness of this volume.

In Spring 1979 Ashbery would spend the weekends with Kermani, and they slowly began to fix up the house in Hudson together, a project that would occupy them for the next few decades. In 1978 Ashbery became art critic at *New York Magazine*. He took up the position to get out of teaching, but the position ended up being 'a terrible job bind', especially since he ended up doing both jobs for two years, which made him feel as if he would 'go out of [his] mind at times';[41] and he did indeed have a 'nervous breakdown' at the magazine one day.[42]

In 1980 Ashbery was offered a job as art critic for *Newsweek*, 'which was much better paid, but in some ways worse, because *Newsweek* is a much bigger magazine', and he regularly had to produce an article on a subject he knew little about.[43] Ashbery lasted six months, during which time he lived in constant fear of prominent elderly artists dying, since it would mean going down to the office at midnight to write an obituary. Ashbery's increasing canonization and accruing of global cultural capital is apparent in a trip sponsored by the United States Information Agency (USIA) to Europe that he embarked on, in May 1980, alongside Susan Sontag and Joyce Carol Oates. Jaroslaw Anders,

Ashbery, *c.* 1977, photographs attributed to Larry Rivers. The photographs were used as a model for Silver's painting 'Pyrography: Poem and Portrait of John Ashbery II'.

a Polish writer who accompanied the group, recalls Ashbery crying at Auschwitz (as Sontag did not).[44] In Poland Ashbery met the Polish poet Piotr Sommer, who had already begun translating his work. In an interview with Sommer in his Warsaw apartment, Ashbery concedes that though he dislikes interviews in principle, he consented to such a long one because Sommer had been a wonderful guide and host during his two-week stay in Poland.[45] Ashbery, on the other hand, notes his pleasure in giving readings: 'Because I like my poetry and I'm willing to promote it, within certain limits.'[46]

The late 1970s and early 1980s were, for Ashbery, a period of readjustment: a new reflective period that is most clearly expressed in 'Litany', the long poem of his 1979 collection *As We Know*. The poem, composed in two columns, was inspired by the work of Elliott Carter: a duo for violin and piano that Ashbery had heard performed at Cooper Union in March 1975, which he recalls as 'a remarkably conversational, or non-conversational, kind of music'.[47] Ashbery was fascinated by the parts, which 'could almost have been in different worlds, except for the fact that they were obviously listening to and spying on each other, each trying to get the upper hand', making the composition symbolic of the practice of collaboration, in particular, and an increasingly private society in general.[48] Ashbery conceives of 'Litany' as two separate poems that demand our attention at the same time, which creates the impression of 'eavesdropping on two different conversations at a cocktail party – something that happens to us all fairly often and therefore should have a poem written about it'.[49] This effect is amplified in a taped recording of the poem that Ashbery made with Ann Lauterbach for Zero Bull Shit (ZBS), an experimental recording studio in Fort Edward, New York, that was founded in 1970 in the midst of the Counterculture movement.

Lauterbach later published an essay on the experience, 'What We Know as We Know It: Reading "Litany" with J. A.', in which she notes how, after it was first recorded, she would play it 'at night, with the lights out, as a fantastic lullaby: my own voice merging and diverging from his, his mine, two uttering instruments playing in tandem', observing that reading Ashbery was 'an *inextricable interfusion*. Like singing along with life'.[50] 'Litany', with its religious title, indicates a shift in mood for Ashbery's work that arises from his new religious phase (he attended Sunday afternoon service at a chapel in the late 1970s). While the title preserves the ambiguity of the meaning of litany as something sacred, it can also suggest a list of complaints or a droning on.

Ashbery wrote most of the poems in *As We Know* in the summer of 1978, about two months after he finished 'Litany'. The summer was, for Ashbery, a depressing period. There is a passage in De Quincey's 'Confessions of an Opium Eater' that he was always reminded of when the season rolled around, filling him with thoughts of death.[51] 'Late Echo', one of the poems that reflects Ashbery's sombre mood, begins accordingly: 'Alone with our madness and favourite flower/ We see that there really is nothing left to write about.'[52] The collection has a particularly morbid air, a theme that continues to be the governing subject of his subsequent collections. Ashbery's move to Hudson inaugurated a significant change in the mood of his poetry, beginning in the 1980s, a mood which is characterized by an alertness to death, a nostalgia and a propensity to self-eulogize, coupled with, as is typical of his desire to break free of any sticky mould, a desire to keep moving away from any definitive position. Ashbery describes his house as very beautiful but also as having a certain kind of 'gloom that one knows'.[53] The house – which was, like his grandparents' house, built in the 1890s – reminded Ashbery of 'the happiest part of my childhood, when I felt secure and taken care of, and was living in a city and had other children to play with'.[54] It was a 'terrible blow' to Ashbery when his grandparents had to sell their house, but in Hudson, he was able to create a remodelling of sorts.[55]

The ornate, colonial-revival house, with restored period wallpaper, Chippendale furniture and stained glass, combined an American and European sophistication – like the kind of residence imagined in a Henry James novel. Its dark, wood-panelled walls and curtained windows added to the gloomy atmosphere; Modernist styles and aesthetics were combined by way of paintings and collectible objects that were visible in the house, including a Jane Freilicher still-life, which lined the walls. The highly stylized effect, in contrast to the simpler decor of his Chelsea apartment, created the feel of being inside one of Ashbery's poems, with their eccentric, continually unravelling space and their periodic indeterminacy.[56] 'Going through the front door was a bit like opening a jewel box,' Winkfield recalls 'something to look at in every nook and cranny'.[57] Ashbery's thinking about architecture was influenced during this period by his reading of Robert Harbison's *Eccentric Spaces* (1977), in which he argues that an architectural space that is 'deliberately decentralised and unfocused' creates a sense of illumination and

Ashbery's Hudson house, 2008.

enchantment.[58] The Hudson house, carefully furnished with chance finds in antique stores collected over the years, was like a large poetic project – the supreme fiction of Ashbery's work, which he endlessly revised (and which now exists as the digital space 'John Ashbery's Nest').[59] During the period when Ashbery lived between New York and Hudson, Kermani, who ran an Albany rug business in these years, noted that he would write poems in New York while preoccupying himself with translation and criticisms upstate.[60]

By the early 1980s Ashbery was aware of how he was being absorbed by a younger generation of poets, and his poems from this period are explicitly addressed to a group of disciples. *Shadow Train* (1981), a collection that was not widely well reviewed and which is often seen as a filler publication, is peopled by follower figures. Written over a nine-month period, the collection is composed of a fifty-poem sequence that Ashbery describes as 'an artificial concept that was loose enough to let me do what I wanted and strict enough to bring me to the task each time I wanted to do it.'[61] Ashbery considers the parody of regular form in the collection 'a kind of antiform, really, a lining up of four stanzas of four lines each', suggesting a model in the minimalist work of artists such as Donald Judd in the 1960s – 'four oblongs next to each other, rather than a hard, humanistic treatment of geometry such as you get in Piet Mondrian. It really is, then, an asymmetry, a coldness, an alteration.'[62] The cold climate of this collection is marked, again, by an atmosphere of distrust, one that might be contextualized within the Reaganite political climate of the early 1980s. 'The silence, as they say,' the artist David Salle, who lived in New York at the time, writes, 'was deafening. No one could believe that this B-actor was about to occupy the White House.'[63] *Shadow Train* gives the air of an emptied vehicle moving in some unknown future direction: the poems are like the carriages of a train – linked, but without any real sense of direction. The reader in the collection is treated, too, like an object of suspicion: far from the early days of an intimate coterie readership, they have to earn the poet's trust when the poet presents himself, as in 'At the Inn', as an enigma: 'Be rebus or me now.'[64]

In 'Joe Leviathan', the reader is invited to 'pass through' the poet: 'He can pass with me in the meaning and we still not see/ ourselves,' Ashbery writes; identity remains forever elusive in his work, and its title suggests how one thing might absorb another without producing something new or leaving an obvious mark of influence.[65] To 'pass through' is a striking way to frame influence, which provides a countermodel to Harold Bloom's theory of the anxiety of influence, orienting tradition's work towards the future rather than the past.[66] The collection also contains 'Paradoxes and Oxymorons', a poem that is not only suggestive of the performance of readership but is one of the most coherent statements on the contradictions and paradoxes that govern Ashbery's ambivalent attitude to poetics: he addresses his reader, 'And the poem/ Has set me softly down beside you. The poem is you.'[67] As late as the galley proofs, Ashbery thought of making 'Paradoxes and Oxymorons' his title poem. He wanted to use the title 'with the photograph I found that I liked very much of a Viennese house which seemed to have overtones of Wittgenstein in it, not only the title but the room itself'.'[68] He decided, however, that the title 'seemed a bit difficult for your average book buyer', revealing a desire to reach the common reader – a pull that was hardly at the centre of the young Ashbery's publishing concerns. Wittgenstein's dictum that 'the meaning of a word is its use in language' perhaps lies behind the speculative and cautionary tone of this collection, where, as in the poem 'Drunken Americans', shadowy presences and glimpses of importance fabricate themselves, without consolidating into something definite:

I saw the reflection in the mirror
And it doesn't count, or not enough
To make a difference[.]⁶⁹

The poems in the collection are private poems: they redefine
the right to privacy at a time when Reagan openly declared that the
gay rights movement's 'alternative lifestyle' was one society could
not condone.⁷⁰ A kind of deflationary rhetoric is one of Ashbery's
weapons in this defence; the other is irony. 'White-Collar Crime' is
a poem that, following a decade of violent crime in New York, for
which it became known as 'Fear City', puts a white liberal hypocrisy
under the microscope: 'His fault wasn't great; it was over-eagerness;
it didn't deserve/ The death penalty, but it's different when it
happens/ In your neighbourhood, on your doorstep' (Reagan was
of the opinion that the 'death penalty saves lives').⁷¹ The vision
of the present articulated in 'Hard Times' (1981), with its nod to
Dickens, is likewise unsparing.⁷² Observing the present moment
from the future, Ashbery writes, 'they will tell you what we've all
known for years:/ That the power of this climate is only to conserve
itself.' The vision of New York as a place of 'crime and sodomy' was
one that made Ashbery's parents 'very suspicious' in the 1950s, but,
in spite of New York's notorious reputation in the 1970s, Ashbery
continued to celebrate the city: 'I love the way New York looks,'
he explained in a 1985 interview, 'the way everything is mashed
together and somehow gives one a sense of elation.'⁷³

7

'The Tribe of John': In the Manner of Ashbery, 1984–94

Ashbery began the composition of his next collection, *A Wave* (1984), in 1982; it was written in the wake of his close encounter with death. In Spring 1982, a staphylococcal infection of the spine came on suddenly while he was delivering a class at Brooklyn College, beginning as paralysis of the neck before taking over his whole body. Although doctors told Kermani that Ashbery would be left quadriplegic, he made a swift recovery (though it left him with an occasional limp), with few recollections of the ordeal he had been through. The collection's long title-poem, 'A Wave', begins, accordingly, 'To pass through pain and not know it.'[1] This encounter with pain governs the poem's 'surreal intimacy', which is, as Ashbery concedes, 'really a love poem . . . written about somebody I was in love with'.[2] Ashbery believed that long poems are 'much closer to a whole reality' than shorter poems.[3] In this one he tries to get at the heady feeling of love, coupled with the temporal sequence that, writing in his later years, he knows is inevitable: 'Forgetting about "love"/ For a moment puts one miles ahead, on the steppe or desert/ Whose precise distance as it feels I / Want to emphasize and estimate.'[4] Love, here, is a wave that inundates. The kernel of the idea for 'A Wave' was prompted by Guercino's *Landscape with Tobias and the Angel*, which Ashbery saw while reviewing an exhibition of Italian Baroque painting in the summer of 1980. The painting, which features a son who gathers a great fish to cure the blindness of his father – in the most Oedipal of narratives – makes the poem not only a love poem but one that is concerned explicitly with the shadowy figure of the father.

References to the painting that are apparent in the first typescript, which bears the title 'Long Periods of Silence', disappear in the second. In their place are references to the flood and its aftermath. A new beginning – marked in the poem as New Year 1983 – is written into the poem: 'The beginning of the arc of the year/ May not gradually melt into rainbow, salmon-hued, messy/ Rainbow extravagances', recalling the ecstatic ending of Elizabeth Bishop's 'The Fish'.[5] In the earlier version of the poem, the son tries to come to terms with the paternal silence. Ashbery's near-death experience perhaps prompted a reflection of his father's death two decades previously, and the long shadow of silence that he had cast on his own life. A shorter poem in the collection, 'Problems', coming directly before 'A Wave', reads as its prelude. Its speaker recalls: 'Once, someone – my father – came to me and spoke/ Extreme words amid the caution of the time.'[6] The poem continues: 'I was too drunk, too scared to know what was being said/ Around us then, only that it was a final/ Shelving off.'

Ashbery was certainly known to drink a lot during this period. The critic Marjorie Perloff recalled various visits from Ashbery to her home in Los Angeles in the late 1970s and '80s, when he would make himself at home with her drinking cabinet, while she prepared dinner, or disappear off into the night with a handsome poet, apologizing profusely afterwards. 'I've always', she recalled him quipping, 'been dependent on the kindness of strangers.'[7] 'A Wave' can be read as a working-through of this state of inebriation, which seems connected to his father's violence, which had long troubled him. In 'A Wave', Ashbery revisits, in dream structure, the father of his childhood, as a way of working through the shame of the 'old man' who 'was gazing at the grass/ As though in sorrow, sorrow for what I had done'.[8] Psychoanalysis might well have prompted this exploration. As Ashbery notes in a 1980 interview,

'Being in the situation, at certain hours of the week, of saying what one has on one's mind undoubtedly influenced my writing . . . I no longer wait around for a "privileged moment."'[9]

In his collaborative interview with Koch, Ashbery associates pain with an act of not knowing that he suggests is intrinsic to the poetic process: 'the idea of relief from pain has something to do with ambiguity. Ambiguity supposes an eventual resolution of itself, whereas certitude implies further ambiguity.'[10] In working through pain, Ashbery ends up not only with a very different idea of who his father was, but a new articulation of his poetics as situated, as he writes in 'But What Is the Reader to Make of This', 'On the outside looking out', a position that gives a scene 'a quarter turn' until the interior separates out from the surrounding drama.[11] Giving a symptom a 'quarter-turn' is how Lacan describes psychoanalytic thought.[12] *A Wave* is written with an urgency of working through a personal and social conundrum; it marks a newfound fulfilment and a culmination of a period of writing. Shortly after completing the collection, Ashbery began compiling his *Selected Poems* (1985), spending time fiddling over its order even if, as he concedes in a 1981 interview, he accepts 'the universal fact that really nobody sits down – I mean maybe there are some people, poetry freaks – and reads a book of poems from beginning to end. I think most people don't. I certainly don't.'[13]

The late 1980s ushered in a new period of rest and relaxation, as Ashbery was awarded a MacArthur Fellowship in 1985, to the sum of $250,000, which he heard about while he was in London. Ever an anglophile, Ashbery had always maintained a close relationship with his English contemporaries – John Ash and Lee Harwood most notably – London being the other corner of the cultural triangle that complements Paris and New York. 'Now I'm going for a tramp on Hampstead Heath though the weather is "threatening,"' Ashbery jots in a postcard to Elmslie. Harwood memorably recalls Ashbery's pull from across the Atlantic in his 1966 poem 'The Man With Blue Eyes':

As your eyes are blue
you move me – and the thought of you –
I imitate you.[14]

Ashbery is perhaps most eloquent on his own work through the
looking glass of his English contemporaries: introducing Ash at
a reading in New York in 1992, he notes how 'his love for the city,
kept in check by his exemplary "disbelief," has produced a body of
poetry in which we recognize ourselves and our neighbourhoods
in a new mirror,' and continues by noting that 'I don't think for a
minute that John functions as a sort of bridge between the mutually
hostile worlds of British and American poetry . . . both countries
would probably sink like Atlantis if they found themselves so
intimately, so embarrassingly connected.'[15] Despite such a lofty
refusal of the idea of the special connection in poetry, Ashbery goes
on to list the pervasive connection between the two nations, and
reflects, listing devastating recent events, on the irony of a recent
news story that claimed New York to be the 'safest city in the world',
in spite of the ongoing AIDS epidemic.

Ashbery's subsequent collection, *April Galleons* (1987), written
in the mid-1980s, is full of poems that eulogize a moment when
the libidinal zones of the city are razed in the service of New York's
1980s neoliberal expansion, a feeling that the writer Samuel Delany
captures in *Times Square Red, Times Square Blue* (1999), a book
that contemplates the social consequences of the Times Square
Development Project. Ashbery echoes these sentiments most
explicitly in 'Forgotten Sex', which opens, 'They tore down the old
movie palaces,/ Ripped up streetcar tracks, widened avenues./
Lampposts, curbs with their trees vanished.'[16] Ashbery experiences
the loss of the movie theatres, which were once the portal to his
imaginative life, with the deepest regret. The vanishing of trees
– the most stable referent of his poetics of intimacy – articulates
the sense of despair that descends on Ashbery during these years.

'Forgotten Sex' articulates the feeling of seeing a neighbourhood gentrified, and the difficulty of mourning not only the loss of a group of friends and contemporaries, but the entire architecture of a community: 'A story of departing hands and affairs, that mostly/ Went untold, unless someone who was there once/ Visited the old neighbourhood.' The poem is one of Ashbery's most outspoken (or as outspoken as Ashbery gets) queer poems, which barely conceals its rage for the lives collapsing around him.

The mid-1980s witnessed the first dawning of the devastation that the AIDS epidemic would reap upon New York's artistic communities, which would shift Ashbery's otherwise causal distance from the gay scene (at least on the page). Although *April Galleons* is often seen as a less successful collection than *A Wave* – or as a bridge to *Flow Chart* – it powerfully captures the silent history of this moment and the difficulty that Ashbery faced in his anti-identitarian queer politics in the face of the increasingly central role that sexual identity assumed in Reaganite America. AIDS revealed, as professor David Bergman writes, that the gay community was powerless to put pressure on not only the Health Department but on other city institutions too, such as the *New York Times* or Mayor Ed Koch, who was rumoured to be gay.[17] AIDS loomed over New York gay social life, and effectively brought an end to the seemingly apolitical stance of the New York School cohort. The working through of this communal trauma lies behind so many of the lyrics of *April Galleons*, a stance that is exemplified in 'Too Happy, Happy Tree', in which Ashbery writes, 'in the silent/ History: how we were all going to be lovers/ When a climatic change occurred'.[18] The line breaks that separate 'silent' from 'History' are suggestive of the subtle ways in which Ashbery's poetry articulates itself around a silenced history, exposing those historical processes.

Much of the poetry written in these years wrestles with how to negotiate the imitative qualities of his work, which attracted flocks of younger poets, and which made Ashbery highly self-conscious of his role as the most important poet of the era. Ashbery had a constant influx of acolytes but, as Perloff notes, it is his vast circle of reference that makes him entirely inimitable.[19] He was, nonetheless, highly generous in his praise of other poets, and would blurb books for whoever asked him to. Ashbery's introduction to *The Best American Poetry 1988*, which he was invited to edit by David Lehman, shows, in an unusually earnest manner, how, reading through the poetry of 1987, he 'was struck, perhaps for the first time, by the exciting diversity, the tremendous power it could have for enriching our lives'.[20]

After a sense of impasse that is felt through the mid-1980s, this immersion in the variety of poetries being written gives Ashbery new momentum to rise to the challenge of poetry's social role. This was facilitated by being awarded a MacArthur, which meant that he could give up work for five years. The new luxury of the fellowship changed Ashbery's writing pace, as he explains in a 1987 interview: 'I used to think that it wasn't good for me to write very often. I thought one a week was perhaps the maximum. Otherwise it seemed as though it was coming out diluted, or strained. However, I seemed to have changed my mind about this, and am writing just about every day. And feeling okay about what I am writing.' He adds that the feeling of ageing creeping up on him, too, prompted this new productivity, 'realising there aren't the oceans of time that seem to be stretching ahead when one was young. And one learns to use it and realise how precious it is.'[21]

Flow Chart, the project that Ashbery was working on during these years, is epic in scope, a book-length poem that is his most consummate project: a reckoning with his own life, and a meditation on the crisis of identity, both personal and American, at a time when the Reagan administration had segued into the George H. W. Bush administration, without any let-up for the queer community. When Winkfield, who would design the book's cover, was motoring with Ashbery on a visit to Hudson that year, he suggested that, to resolve the writer's block Ashbery had had since his mother's death, he write about her, and the thoughts and memories triggered by her passing. Though Ashbery said he 'would never do anything so obvious', his mother does 'occasionally make a cameo appearance' and is a kind of centrifugal centre of the expansive poem.[22] Her passing is delivered with characteristic wit: 'a niche in time, and she, too, preferred not to get out of it.'[23] Winkfield's premise becomes another constraint of sorts that fuels this poem about writing a life and a life in writing (Ashbery, Winkfield and Mathews were united in their deep passion for Roussel's work, with its complex puzzles and constraints). Imposing another constraint on himself, Ashbery decided that he would stop writing the poem on his sixtieth birthday, but, in fact, concedes that he ran out of steam a little before, at the beginning of July 1987, and set it aside, knowing that such writing, done so long at a high energy level, would require substantial revisions.

The friendship between Winkfield and Ashbery, who collaborated on a *livre d'artiste* in 1998, was typical of the relationship between the New York literary and visual art worlds in the 1980s and '90s. Winkfield first heard Ashbery read 'The Skaters' at the U.S. Embassy in London in 1965, which prompted his initial communication, and after Winkfield's move to New York in 1976, the two became friends, and continued to make cameo-appearances in each other's work.[24] When Ashbery was hospitalized in 1982, Winkfield presented him with a canvas, with the title 'Fragment' on the back, noting: 'this, my first canvas in seventeen years, for John Ashbery abed, May 1982'. In a 1986 review of one of Winkfield's exhibitions, Ashbery delightfully describes his work as 'though Bosch and Beatrix Potter had collaborated on a Book of Hours', writing that, 'it is important to note the literary connection' since this literariness (in contrast to much of contemporary art) 'may be one reason why his previous New York shows attracted so little attention', another being that 'it's impossible to put a label on his work', both of which were anathema

Trevor Winkfield, *Fragment*, 1982, acrylic on canvas.

to the art world in the 1980s, and the signature of greatness for
Ashbery.[25] No longer forced to attend every art gallery opening
around town, Ashbery spent his evenings in the late 1980s watching
'hundreds of bad movies' recorded from late-night television,
including the *Mexican Spitfire* series, *A Great Gildersleeve* and low-
budget noir films like *Detour*. He also collected films of Edward D.
Wood Jr, 'the worst film director ever', who made *Glen or Glenda?*,
perhaps Hollywood's first film about transvestism.[26]

In May 1989 Ashbery was invited by a Japanese professor to
visit Japan on a reading tour, and he took Kermani along with him.
Ashbery had always been interested in Japanese culture: *A Wave*
contains a series of four haibuns – short, essay-like prose pieces,
usually accompanied by a haiku, which Ashbery had learnt about
from the anthology of Japanese poetry Hiroaki Sato translated with
Burton Watson in 1981. Ashbery was a fan, too, of Yasujirō Ozu's
films, several of which he saw at MoMA, noting that one of Ozu's
titles, *I Was Born, but . . .* is how he felt about his own life history.[27]

'Ah Kyoto! Home of blowfish and Haagen-Daaz,' Ashbery quips in a 1992 letter, delighting as ever in finding a dash of Americana where one expects it least.[28] While in Japan, Ashbery delivered a lecture at Shirayuri Women's University in Tokyo on the suggested topic of 'Poetic Phenomenology and Ashbery himself', which later became his essay 'Poetical Space'. In the talk, he remarks how poetry is, even more so than painting, free to make up its own rules. A poem, he writes, making a case for the distinctiveness of his medium, 'can "put a girdle round the earth in forty minutes"– even technology has a hard time keeping pace with that', emphasizing that 'poetry is not a stationary object but a kinetic act'; a space of connection 'in which something is transferred from somebody to somebody else'.[29] Back in the USA, the culture wars were in full flow. Though many of the poems in *April Galleons* seem preoccupied with the idea of conservation in an abstract way, Ashbery's introduction to Mapplethorpe's *Pistils* recalls the well-known controversy that surrounded Mapplethorpe's 1989 exhibition 'The Perfect Moment'. Ashbery, typically, makes his commentary on Mapplethorpe's 'lurid depictions of violent sex' by way of his erotic flower photographs, the 'tip of the iceberg', which was the queer cultural position that he himself assumed. It is an essay that evokes the scandals of the time and the repressive cultural moment that, while nowhere central in Ashbery's own work, can be felt in his own modes of forgetting, evading and holding off: 'Like fig leaves for absent genitalia, they point to the scandal of what is not there.'[30]

Ashbery set *Flow Chart* aside for two years and returned to it between 1989 and 1990, as he was delivering his Charles Norton Lectures at Harvard. In these lectures, which focused on six poets that had proved influential to his own trajectory, he outlines his own eccentric tradition of minor poets. Ashbery opens the lectures by alluding to what he expects to be demanded of him: to '"spill the beans," so to speak' on his own work.[31] Characteristically eschewing any such invitation, he offers his readers instead a key to his work through contextual and close readings of an unlikely grouping of Anglo-French-American poets: John Clare, Thomas Lovell Beddoes, Raymond Roussel, John Wheelwright, Laura Riding and David Schubert. In associating his own work with this idiosyncratic collection of writers, Ashbery is also implicitly positing an alternative to the more traditional line of poets in which Harold Bloom had canonized him. We are presented with six snapshots of Ashbery through the prism of these poets. Though always resistant to naming his own autobiographical referents, it is clear in this collection of portraits that Ashbery is interested in the life story of poets and sees them as enriching their work. The lectures opened with Auden's provocation in *Nineteenth-Century British Minor Poets*, in which he makes a case for the false distinction between minor and major poets. Not all of the subjects (most of whom were long dead) approved of the grouping, however, and, in fact, Riding made a particular objection to her inclusion with this mixed bunch, which Ashbery suggests might be on account of Wheelwright's negative review of two of Riding's collections in *Poetry*. Though delighting in poets' gossip, Ashbery is more interested, donning his pseudo-psychoanalyst's hat, in drawing our attention to the uncanny similarity of their work. Or, as he quotes Wheelwright on Riding, 'It is fun to recognize friends in masquerade. There is fun in masquerade itself, even though personages, when recognized, turn out to be enemies or bores, or to be scarcely persons at all.'[32]

Staying in one of the Harvard houses, which had a view of Memorial Drive and the Charles River, similar to the one he had as a student, awoke 'many long slumbering memories', and the revisions to *Flow Chart* were prompted by this re-encounter with his youth.[33] The autobiographical template that Ashbery had rehearsed in 'Soonest Mended' becomes, in the huge mnemonic surge of *Flow Chart*, a way of articulating 'the bloodstream of our collective memory', a project that Ashbery also explicitly suggests is directed towards an articulation of a marginal position that becomes

the secret untold history, a history that was ever present as AIDS
continued to wreak destruction on American life:[34]

> It occurs to me in my home on the beach
> sometimes that others must have experiences identical to mine
> and are also unable to speak of them, that if we cared
> enough to go into each other's psyche and explore
> around, some of the canned white entrepreneurial brain food
> could be reproduced in time to save the legions
> of the disposed . . . [35]

Ashbery, parodying the prophetic mode of the bard in his most
autobiographical poem, refuses the idea of individuality, which
lies behind the whole notion of an autobiographical project. Our
experiences, he suggests, are not unique but rather 'identical', and
the role of the poet is valuable insofar as he can perform the role of
analyst for his community, giving voice to what others cannot speak
of and, in this way, resisting the 'canned white entrepreneurial
brain food' that had become symptomatic of the neoliberal
moment. Part of the way in which Ashbery distances himself from
his own individuality is in serving as a medium for other voices:
'I'm more someone else, taking dictation/ from on high, in a
purgatory of words.'[36] As everywhere in Ashbery's work, there is
always a note of comedy that accompanies any proclamation of his
role as bard, a comedy that, as Perloff maintains, has been greatly
underestimated.[37]

    Flow Chart is not only very long – at 5,000 lines it is one of the
longest poems written by an American poet – but it makes use, for
the most part, of long lines, a form which recalls that of 'The Skaters'.
The poem's serpentine divagations and experimental turns channel
the strong emotional currents that are prompted by the thought of
death, in general, and by his mother's death in particular. The poem's
strong flow enfolds various tones, combining political registers

('Latest reports show that the government/ still controls everything'),
the force of the market ('Despite handicaps trading continues'), a
parodic take on artistic success ('Repetition makes reputation . . .
You need no longer inspect the materials/ when you buy them in
bulk') and the insufficiency of language ('Words, however are not
the culprit. They are at worst a placebo/ leading nowhere').[38] 'We're
interested in the language, that you call breath,' Ashbery writes in a
double sestina in the poem (its long lines and pliable shape contain
a variety of poetic forms).[39] The poem is, nonetheless, an exploration
of what language reveals about our contemporary world; a way of
resisting the pull of the academy with its penchant for Francophile
thought ('The French still say "hailstones big as pigeon's/ eggs"')
and the routine language of cultural contemporaneity (the poets 'are
retreating into–or is it out of?–academia').[40] As Charles Bernstein
recalls, the publication of John Shoptaw's homotextual study of
Ashbery's work *On the Outside Looking Out* (1994), a landmark study
of Ashbery's entire body of work up until that point, was met with
ambivalence by Ashbery, who expressed his reservations about
Shoptaw's reading of him as a gay poet, which he saw as potentially
reductive if it were to become the primary frame.[41]

Ashbery's father makes another appearance in this poem as
his 'biological father' whose rage is tempered by irony: he 'got
mad/ and went out and I didn't see him for thirty years, by which
time both of us had aged/ considerably but were still reasonably
attractive'.[42] *Flow Chart* pulls back towards an insistent ordinary
dailiness, absorbing these significant and traumatic moments
into its flow, with a touch of humour, so that the 'feeling/ of
emptiness' sits in tension with 'Most days are well fed/ and
relaxing,' as Ashbery's were during this period.[43] The poem reflects
on various American decades, giving us a personalized (though
oddly impersonalized) feel for the time: 'In the sixties new dresses
were newer./ The humbler children were clad in dimity, and bird-
cheerful. Airlines seldom/ overbooked.'[44]

When his MacArthur grant ended, Ashbery was appointed Professor of Languages and Literature at Bard College, a position he held until 2008: he taught on Fridays and would spend the weekends browsing antique shops in upstate New York for further ornaments to fill his Hudson abode. The pace of this life enters the composition of *Flow Chart*, a nostalgic tone that reminisces on life outside the metropolis when 'It seems only yesterday/ that one could find cheap walkup apartments in the East 50s and modest restaurants/ such as the Cloisters, with $1.95 complete lunches, or luncheons'; and in which he stages the disappearance of a 'precious notebook' that would have contained 'something like/ my autobiography', which would, as he notes, 'have falsified/ everything'.[45] 'Nostalgia, if it isn't good for anything else, seems to elicit poetry,' Ashbery notes in a 1994 essay, 'The Poet's Hudson River Restoration', published in *Architectural Digest*.[46]

After Ashbery finished his Norton lectures at Harvard, he embarked upon another USIA-sponsored trip to Yugoslavia, Sweden and the Soviet Union, again accompanied by Kermani. The trip, made against the backdrop of the fall of the Iron Curtain, put an end to the Cold War atmosphere that had shaped Ashbery's early work.

After 'a few bleak years review-wise in the U.S.', Ashbery welcomed the positive reviews of *Flow Chart*.[47] His subsequent collection, *Hotel Lautréamont* (1992), which collates the shorter lyrics that he wrote while completing his long, effusive work, is as static in its conception as *Flow Chart* is free-flowing. These heavily formalized poems create a sense of enclosure and isolation that is reinforced by their regular repetitions and held together through the poem's central metaphor of the hotel. The hotels of Ashbery's main personal experiences that he recollects are the dingy ones he resided in on first moving to Paris, but the increasing travel that came by way of his growing international status as a poet meant that he was transient a large part of each year. The collection, which is dedicated to Martory, also suggests that Ashbery was reflecting on his years in Paris during the writing of this volume, with its allusion to the self-stylized French poet, Comte de Lautréamont. The precise, preordained structure of the book creates the impression of being locked within one of Joseph Cornell's shadow boxes. Explaining his choice of title in an interview, Ashbery elucidates:

> there is something very attractive about a hotel because
> it has got so many rooms and so many different kinds
> of people all doing different things . . . I thought of the
> four sections of four stanzas each as being like four floors
> of a hotel, like the desk where the keys are hung.

Ashbery notes that he had always been fascinated by houses – hotels being a kind of house – 'Especially houses in America in older parts of cities. They seem to have a commanding presence somehow. They're telling you something.'[48]

The collection is generous and inclusive, yet also suffused with a sense of isolation: 'Dear ghost, what shelter/ in the noonday crowd?' the first poem in the collection, 'Light Turnouts', opens.[49] These poems are like 'safe houses': they are both a refuge from the world and a way of imagining 'a whole cast of characters' as 'imaginary'. The poems' dramatization of their inability to find a suitable interlocutor to make communication happen demonstrates that Ashbery had arrived at a new crisis point, or at least a poetic rut. We might read the poems, as Ashbery writes of Roussel's work in a 1991 article for *Atlas Anthology 7*, which accompanied his translation of Roussel's *Documents pour servir de canevas*, as 'Chinese-box tales with the understanding that we are not being told all; that behind their polished surface an encrypted secret probably exists.'[50] 'How to Continue', the final poem in the collection, breaks out of the tightly enclosed mould of the other poems in the book. Set on the New York piers, the famous site of cruising in the 1950s and '60s, it is an elegy both for a community destroyed by AIDS and for the queer life that arose in these liminal urban spaces:

> And then one day the ship sailed away
> There were no more dreamers just sleepers
> in heavy attitudes on the dock
> moving as if they knew how[.][51]

Ashbery travelled to Australia in 1992 with Kermani, renewing his friendship with John Tranter, who notes that Ashbery gives Australia its own literary effect in 'Tangled Star' (from his collection *Wakefulness*). Tranter recalls how Ashbery

> recited to (him) – at the end of a rather long evening – the epic [nineteenth-century Scottish doggerel poet William] McGonagall poem about the River Tay disaster in 1879. In full, and with rolling eyes and a resolute attempt at the Scots accent: a marvellous performance.[52]

As Perloff recollects, 'he talked the way he wrote.'[53]

The following year Ashbery returned to France upon being named Chevalier de l'Ordre des Arts et des Lettres by the French Ministry of Education and Culture. The award was presented by the French Minister of Culture, Jack Lang, during a reception at Harry Mathews's Paris apartment on the rue de Grenelle. Ashbery spent the year translating Martory's poems in *The Landscape Is Behind the Door*, which was published in 1994.

In Ashbery's subsequent collection, *And the Stars Were Shining*, published later that year, time's relentless passage permeates a collection that is tenderly unsentimental about the inevitable encroachment of age: 'Yet the tree treats me like a brute friend,' the first poem of the collection, 'Token Resistance', closes, with its nod to Rimbaud, 'my own shoes have scarred the walk I've taken.'[54] There is, too, a new hopefulness about community that is articulated in the penultimate section of its title poem:

> I've told you before how afraid this makes me,
> but I think we can handle it together,
> and this is as good a place as any
> to unseal my last surprise[.][55]

The ongoing devastation of AIDS, the soft power of America's cultural diplomacy, the continuation of the neoliberal turn under Clinton and the pretensions of poetry continued to be the subject of Ashbery's late work. In 'The Decline of the West', included in an April 1992 letter to Mark Ford, we find, accordingly, an unusually excoriating mode of irony: 'What! Our culture in its dotage!/ Yet this very poem refutes it,/ springing up out of the collective unconscious/ like a weasel through a grating.'[56] Avant-garde culture still, thankfully, lived on in music at least. In June 1994 WNYC FM's fiftieth anniversary concert, broadcast on the air live from the Lincoln Center in New York, featured twelve composers, including Laurie Anderson, Philip Glass and Milton Babbitt, who responded to Ashbery's poem 'No Longer Very Clear'. Ashbery, for whom experimental music had been so important in formulating his own poetic styles, was given the musical homage his work deserved. In his 1994 piece in *Architectural Digest*, he suggests that his personal life had, too, entered a new period of prosperity: 'I've successfully collaged two nostalgias,' he observes, referring both to his poetic style and to his continued movements between his Chelsea and Hudson abodes.[57]

8

'Jump-Start Variety': The Zaniness of the Late Style, 1994–2017

The desire to communicate is made the explicit subject of Ashbery's longest collection, *Can You Hear, Bird* (1995), which, organized alphabetically by poem title, returns to the tight Oulipian schematic style of his earlier work. In a 1987 interview with Harry Mathews, Ashbery suggests, while coyly denying his use of formal devices, that the benefit of such constraints or schemes is that they allow you to 'get a realism, a sort of casual, unbutton quality . . . an extraordinary limpidity'.[1] In 'The Problem of Anxiety', one of the less opaque poems in the collection, the poet turns fully frontally to readers and asks us what we would do in his place:

> Suppose this poem were about you, would you
> put in the things I've carefully left out[?][2]

The poem concludes with 'the glass eye that stares' at the poet 'in amazement', which alludes, most obviously, to Ralph Waldo Emerson's transparent eyeball and, less obviously, to Bishop's grandmother's glass eye – of poetry not as the space of representation but of vision.[3] If subjects are something that still seem elusive to Ashbery's poetry, his late work is chock-full of data: 'Discordant Data', to borrow the title of one of his poems from his 1998 collection *Wakefulness*. These poems luxuriate in the vertiginous feeling of living through a media age.[4] The poems in *Wakefulness* are, like their predecessors, jaunty, dreamlike and urbane; they reproduce the oddities of contemporary speech and articulate the anxious states we live in. The poems, which read as feedback loops on the noise of the present, might be seen, as Ashbery writes in a review of environmental art, as traversing 'humanist visions' and 'the dark, private, neurotic ones that most of us, unfortunately, feel most at home with'.[5] 'This is not', as one reviewer of *Wakefulness* notes, 'a poetry of the right words in the right order', but a poetry that seeks, in line with the ambition of its title, to make the reader alive to the strange technological landscape and effects that are emerging around us.[6]

As the 1990s sped on towards the millennium, the optimism of the early Clinton years gave way to an acceptance that democratic reforms would be, if less culturally conservative than the former Republican administrations, suffused with a neoliberal spirit. 'Today, a day that makes very little sense', Ashbery writes in his 1998 poem 'Like America'.[7] The sense of crisis that builds up before the turn of the century, coupled with the emergence of new, ever more incessant productivity and precarious kinds of labour, is the subject of his book-length poem 'Girls on the Run' (1999), or 'running into capitalism', to borrow the title of one of its reviews.[8] Characteristically for Ashbery, the social commentary on the present is distanced through the prism of the poem's ostensible subject: the work of the outsider artist Henry Darger. Darger's *In the Realms of the Unreal* is an epic work that Ashbery first encountered in Lausanne in 1996; with canvases and watercolours that frequently reach over 3 metres (10 ft) long, the work is composed from remodelled images, magazines and comics that create a vast tapestry of a make-believe world which follows its heroines, the Vivian Girls, who are engaged in a four-and-a-half-year war against the militarized adults, the Glandelinian Army.

In a *New York Times* interview, deflecting from either a direct explanation of Darger's influence, or the social and political

Ashbery's 70th birthday party, 1997.

context of the work, Ashbery suggests that the work resonated, in particular, since he was fascinated by young girls as a boy and spent his childhood engrossed in Nancy Drew books, the Oz Books and comics like *Little Orphan Annie*. *Girls on the Run*, he explains, was 'a way of accessing that sort of lost paradise'.[9] Darger's worlds are so rich and dense that they beggar the idea of mimesis and, in this way, their ostensibly violent childish subjects, which disarm the viewer, mask Ashbery's true interest in the work: its creation of an entire world unto itself and its total disregard for a canonical artistic tradition. Darger's work becomes a kind of interlocutor for the ungraspable reality that Ashbery seeks to capture in his dark toy-chest of a book, which features a group of girls in a Rimbaudian landscape. The perspective starts out of focus and never settles, so that we are left with a series of violent and otherworldly images of innocence run amok, as Ashbery creates his own version of Darger's armies of Vivian Girls, who are constantly under attack by enemy forces.

Many volumes of shorter poems followed in the 2000s, each coming fast on the heels of the last and posing its own contemporary conundrum to the reader. These late works begin to attract criticism for their 'incoherence', profuseness and generalities.[10] But there is a clarity and a reflectiveness amid this seemingly incessant outpouring. As Perloff observes in a 2001 review,

> these poems are more relaxed, more humorous, more willing to let it all hang out than were those in, say, *The Double Dream of Spring* or *Self-Portrait in a Convex Mirror*. Memory has become increasingly obsessive, playfulness and camp more acceptable, and dialogue with a 'you' who is a close friend or lover becomes the normal lyric mode as does the telling of tales that invokes a shared past.[11]

Two central poems about his youth – 'This Room' and 'The History of My Life' – feature in Ashbery's 2001 collection *Your Name Here*. In *Chinese Whispers* (2002), he returns to the idea of pushing sense as close as it comes to nonsense poetry: 'who/ was hanged last Saturday week for drowning herself in a shower of feathers?' to give a taste of this mode which incorporates citation and pastiche that is more diffuse and generalized than ever before.[12] In a 1993 review of Mark Ford's first collection of poetry, *Landlocked*, Ashbery notes how 'the common reader of poetry, assuming he or she exists, relishes nonsense only when it is clearly labelled as such.'[13] His late style delights in this logic-less storytelling, in anthropomorphized animals and zany poetic productions. In *Where Shall I Wander* (2005), the speaker interpolates the reader in the midst of their daily activities: 'Attention, shoppers,' as one poem in the collection opens, and the reader instantly recognizes Ashbery's distinctive voice – even as it comes in the form of a mall announcement – for no one else writes in this form of dazzling boredom and disarming banality.[14] Poetry, here, rather than shying away from the voice of official culture, slants it until it takes on a heady surreal cast, delivering the breaking news of the American present.

A Worldly Country (2007) continues this dissonance of the times in which we live, conveying the oddity of feeling like a foreigner in one's native land. In his later years, Ashbery was averse to travel, by plane at least, and the worldly country is one that he would have to experience imaginatively – from the perspective of his Hudson abode.[15] The collection's title poem seems to pre-empt the financial crash that would unravel the subsequent year: 'There was no peace in the bathroom, none in the china closet/ or the banks, where no one came to make a deposit./ In short all hell broke loose that wide afternoon.'[16] The collection is dedicated to his friend Barbara Epstein, the former editor of the *New York Review of Books*, whom Ashbery recalls meeting on the stairs leading to the Widener Library's poetry room at Harvard University in Autumn 1945. Ashbery describes Barbara as his first critic (this was before he had met Koch and O'Hara), who advised him to 'lighten up a little as a poet'.[17] Lightness was also the flavour of Ashbery's translation of Pierre Reverdy's short story *Haunted House*, which was published in 2015. Ashbery distinguishes Reverdy's work from Surrealism: 'far from banishing poetry to the unconscious, he lets it move freely in and out of the conscious and unconscious,' which creates a 'moving and lifelike' effect.[18] Ashbery also made the acquaintance of the Canadian film-maker Guy Maddin that year (they had previously been fans of one another's work) and performed the role of narrator in one of his 'live' productions, *Brand upon the Brain!*, in New York. The two subsequently collaborated on an adaptation of the lost Dwain Esper exploitation film *How to Take a Bath*, for which Maddin filmed Ashbery's script. Maddin observes that 'I suppose this gluey and scissory medium is where the sensibilities of [our] chosen fields come closest, where we unroll for the public the secret blueprints for the little visual collisions.'[19]

In 2008, Ashbery retired from his position of Professor Emeritus of Languages and Literature at Bard College, which had become largely honorary during its final decade, though the end of his appointment was met with sadness. [20] Over the next decade his life would be largely confined to the immediate radius of his Hudson home and to Kermani's caring duties. As he quipped in an email to Perloff, sent three days before his death, 'Did you ever see the movie *Whatever Happened to Baby Jane?* If so, you have some idea of what my life is like.'[21] That year, the first solo exhibition of Ashbery's collages, made from 1948 to 2008, was held at Tibor de Nagy gallery in New York (other solo and group shows followed in later years). The production of these collages parallels the intense poetic production of his later years. The elements that make up the works are usually fairly simple: the ground is often a postcard or a scene from a children's book or a cut-out from a vintage magazine. There is something homely about these objects, even at their most subversive: 'They're light and slight,' as a *New York Times* reviewer notes. 'They feel more like keepsakes than like art objects, souvenirs of a life and career that gain interest primarily – some might say entirely – within the context of that life and career.'[22] Background elements include children flying across the Alps, people on go-carts, Dutch men in bowlers, a Hollywood cut-out and a parrot against an electric-blue desert storm and a snakes and ladders board with various cut-outs that is dedicated to Brainard.

After Brainard's death in 1994, Ashbery recovered an envelope of paper cuttings that Brainard had collected for collage use. The envelope was a posthumous message for Ashbery that reminded him of the collages they had made while spending time together in the 1970s. Some of Ashbery's collages were assembled from elements given to him on his birthdays by Brainard. Ashbery's late collage *Popeye Steps Out – for Joe Brainard* (2016) retains much of Brainard's, and indeed Ashbery's, wry, wild playfulness, with every square of a pastoral puzzle game overlaid with a figure from various cartoon, literary, magazine and comic scenes. Ashbery returned to collage form in his late years, making a host of eclectic and subversive images that draw upon his long-held fascination with cartoons, children's picture books, films, homoerotic symbolism, kitsch and heterosexual lifestyles. The power of his collages (much like his poetry) derives from the collision of an improbable conjunction of elements that dazzle and charm the reader without revealing precisely what is occurring in the scene or its significance. In one of the recent collages, *Still Life* (2016) – commenting, or indeed riffing, on his own life and art – a statuesque hand cradling a bunch of grapes is placed in the foreground of Parmigianino's *Self-Portrait in a Convex Mirror*. Ashbery never ceased shifting the grounds of the real.

In October 2008 the Library of America published Ashbery's *Collected Poems, 1956–1987*, edited by Mark Ford (a second volume would follow in 2017), who had become an important interlocutor during the last three decades of Ashbery's life; it was the first volume in the Library of America's collected volumes by a living poet. Reflecting on the publication, Ashbery notes that

> some early poems sound as though I wrote them recently, except for a kind of depth or background that they lack. But certainly some ancient lines are ones I could have written today, like that last line of my 1953 poem 'Popular Songs': 'The actors prepare their first decline.' I love that line and I still like the poem a lot. All it needed was a few decades of transparent overlay.[23]

He includes among his favourites 'He', 'Idaho', 'Eclogue', 'Rain', 'The Chateau Hardware', 'Description of a Masque', 'Alone in the Lumber Business' and 'The Young Prince and the Young Princess'.

In the mid- to late 2000s, Ashbery made friends with young acolytes including Timothy Donnelly and Adam Fitzgerald. Ashbery not only continued to be the unassailable centre of the poetry world but the go-to father figure who would write generous book blurbs for a young generation of emergent poets. *Planisphere*, published in 2009, draws its title from Andrew Marvell's poem 'The Definition of Love', in which two perfect lovers are kept apart by fate, since their perfection would be its ruin. The conceit of the planisphere – like the self-convex mirror – flattens a three-dimensional globe into a two-dimensional one. The titles of the poems in the collection, like those in *Can You Hear, Bird*, are arranged in alphabetical order, creating the sense of an A to Z guide to life (Ashbery never ceased to take pleasure in bringing poetry close to the prosaicness of a user's manual). The poems are also a wry dark-humoured take on the ability to master time, as in 'Uptick', a poem that does its own disappearing act:

> poetry dissolves in
> brilliant moisture and reads us
> to us.[24]

In Spring 2009 the Harvard Film Archive presented 'John Ashbery at the Movies', a series of films curated in celebration of reciprocal influences between film and Ashbery's work. The programme sought to explore not only the active role of film in Ashbery's work but his own illuminating prose on cinema, which includes his essays on Jacques Rivette, whose work 'seems to mark a turning point in the evolution of the art of the film', and who 'never completely turns the tables and so keeps his spectator enthralled, wedding guest-like'. The programme also included the phenomenon of Fantômas, 'everybody's favourite cheapo film noir', Edgar Ulmar's *Detour* and Val Lewton's *The Seventh Victim*, which Ashbery first came across at Harvard, a few years after its 1943 release, and which creates 'a haunting New York ambience, though they were shot thousands of miles away'.[25] Rather than simply referring to film, poems like 'A Lonedale Operator', published in *A Wave* in 1984, enact and inspire the whole experience of cinema-going that was particular to children born in the 1920s before the arrival of television began recycling Hollywood's archives. Spotting a gap in the market of poems written about 'the all-important subject of the first movie they ever saw', 'A Lonedale Operator' recounts Ashbery's enthrallment on viewing, with his grandmother, the Walt Disney cartoon *The Three Little Pigs*, 'back in the days when you went "downtown"'.[26] The experience of cinema-going becomes a way to reflect on the primacy of experience; Ashbery's poetry continually strives to recapture a childish receptiveness that he later experiences with a mature distance: 'I still can't help feeling that I was right the first time, when I was still relatively unencumbered by my experience.'[27] Ashbery began collaborating the following year on Maddin's feature film *The Forbidden Room* (2015) and his 2016 interactive film project *Seances*.

In 2011 Ashbery published his translation of Rimbaud's *Illuminations*, which became the finalist for the Oxford-Weidenfeld Translation Prize (his *Collected French Translations* would be published as a two-volume set in 2014). The significance of Rimbaud's work on Ashbery's poetry can be traced to the beginnings of his career, and in conversation with Adam Fitzgerald he notes that it was the only text that he could think of that he wanted 'to translate for the joy of translating it' (he is 'very much against canonic rules' when translating, or indeed anywhere else).[28] Ashbery continued to be as prolific as he was lauded in his final decade: in 2006 New York City designated 7 April as John Ashbery Day; he was named 'Icon' for LGBT History month in 2011 (an honorary title he doubtless regarded with a certain amount of suspicion, given his resentment of 'the notion that gay writers are sort of expected to talk about sex or their sex lives in public') and received a National Humanities Medal that was presented by President Barack Obama at the White House in February 2012.[29]

In his opening remarks, Obama quoted from Emily Dickinson's poem 'I dwell in Possibility'. Writing about the event for Poetry

Society of America, Darrel Alejandro Holnes remarks that Ashbery appeared 'cordial and visibly joyful as he received his medal'.[30] In *Quick Question* (2012), which was published that year and which is dedicated to Freilicher (a testament to their long-standing friendship), Ashbery presents a series of entertaining New York scenes. The collection, written under the influence of *Illuminations*, shares its mysterious and melodramatic sweep, moving from the intimate to the cinematic: 'She was startling in her new headdress,' he writes in 'The Bicameral Eyeball'; 'Oodles of trolls performed the funeral litany.'[31] Then he returns to poetry in the form of an American newsreel: 'Somewhere in America someone is trying to figure out/ how to pay for this.'[32] The reader of the poem is a passenger on a bus that 'goes', like the past, 'down Woodrow Wilson Avenue' (Ashbery's poems are insistently circular, returning to moments when progressive reform agendas were envisaged), alluding to America's twentieth-century president who argued for governmental intervention in the banking system, writing at a moment when that question had taken on a new urgency.

The exhibition 'John Ashbery Collects', co-curated by Adam Fitzgerald and Emily Skillings, based on his Hudson house, was held in Autumn 2013 at Loretta Howard Gallery in New York. The show built upon earlier examinations of Ashbery's home and surroundings, in particular, 'Created Spaces: John Ashbery's Textual and Domestic Environments', a group of essays that appeared in *Rain Taxi* in 2008. Collecting had always been a central aesthetic principle of Ashbery's work; the exhibition made a strong case for the importance of the domestic in his writing. In her essay 'Hudson 1993: A Tour of John Ashbery's Home', the poet Rosanne Wasserman, who edited Ashbery's French translations with Eugene Richie, recalls how she wrote many poems about or including elements of the house when she stayed there in the early 1990s, noting that she was not alone in the endeavour – that many poets and artists who were guests in Hudson found themselves equally

Ashbery, January 2015, photograph by Grant Delin.

moved to write, record and respond to the rich and idiosyncratic spaces they found themselves in. For Wasserman, Ashbery's home, full of curios, had the opposite effect to a museum collection insofar as its 'subtle, funny, and magnificent scenarios' are treated as part of the landscape where one gets on with the dishes and the ordinary business of living. 'One of the most beautiful works inspired by the house', she notes, 'has been the composer Robin Holloway's *Violin Concerto, Opus 70*. When someone once complimented John on this effect, he grinned and troped Falstaff – "I am not only poetic in myself, but the cause that poetry is in other men!"'[33] As Ann Lauterbach has observed, 'His greatness has allowed many poets – from David Lehman to, say, Charles Bernstein, to name two not quite at random – to explore the territory he opened.'[34]

In his introduction to a celebratory reading of Ashbery at Pioneer Works in New York in 2015, in Ashbery's 88th year, the poet Ben Lerner observes how

> reading some of the recent poems is like eavesdropping on conversations in an alien world a lot like this one – as if a change in an intergalactic wind enabled us to overhear the telenovelas and advertisements and small talk of a sister civilization from which ours was separated at birth.[35]

Ashbery's final collections, *Breezeway* (2015) and *Commotion of the Birds* (2016), are suffused with the sayings of imaginary worlds; clichés that resonate anew as clichés, with a strangely familiar effect, as if we sensed a universal grammar underlying the oddity of our contemporary world. In these late collections, Ashbery stays true to the myriad wry voices that light up his brain so that, as he tells us in 'By Guess and by Gosh' (2014), 'You get Peanuts and War and Peace/ some in rags, some in jags, some in/ velvet gown.'[36] The surface of the poems is flat, the tones zany, the transitions between lines unbounded, announcing the whiplash of our technological consciousness; but the idioms are so formally expansive that they create a sonic resonance of their own – a new kind of understanding; a new hold on a very contemporary reality. In this vein, 'Seven-Year-Old Auroch Likes This' gives us:

> Thanks
> to a snakeskin toupee, my grayish push boots
> exhale a new patina/prestige. Exeunt the Kardashians.[37]

'Exeunt the Kardashians' is quite an exit for a Harvard-educated poet, born in the 1920s, the darling of Helen Vendler and Harold Bloom. Ashbery's own meme-filled poetic landscape is a world away from the reticence of *Some Trees*, and yet every principle of his early work's drive to abstraction, combined with a desire to get close to the language of the 'pure products of America', has involved a continual uncanny absorption of the American vernacular, replete with Fox News journalese, *Teen Vogue* advice and *West Wing* political spin. His vast body of work has, over an eighty-year period, assimilated the strange passing shapes of culture, making the post-war poem into something unrecognizable to itself: a thermometer, a heart valve, a speedometer of our zany, and increasingly uninhabitable, contemporary landscape.

In June 2017 Ashbery was awarded the Raymond Roussel Society medal, which was an edible version of the souvenir that Roussel kept from his visit to Camille Flammarion. His health did not permit him to receive it in person, and Winkfield accepted it on his behalf.[38] Winkfield recalls that when presented with the medal at his home in Hudson, 'he extracted the specially baked star cookie from its gold container and woofed [*sic*] it down', the perfect anecdote for the esoteric pleasures of his poetry, of a life's learning, an all-consuming life's work.[39]

Epilogue: 'Let's Pay Attention': Ashbery's Afterlives

As Ashbery turned ninety in July 2017, the artist Daniel Brian Jones contacted a group of poets, musicians and artists, Ashbery included, to create an audio recording of *Flow Chart*, a testament to its continual significance for a contemporary generation of poets. Ashbery's death the following month, on 3 September, brought with it an outpouring of grief and waves of tributes from the national and international poetic and artistic community. Never, it seemed, had a poet been so popular in widely different poetic communities, or expressed something so distinctive about the present – an expansive one for a poet who wrote profusely over eight decades. Long-time friends and fellow artists gathered to express their own sense of what the most important American poet of the twentieth century meant to them. Lyn Hejinian writes movingly of the central place of death in Ashbery's work, which she locates as early as the stubborn virtuousness of 'Little J. A.': 'he was one of the greatest poets of human history,' she writes, 'his own history (the future of his work) is yet to come.'[1] Ann Lauterbach recollects how Ashbery the man – 'a person of rare traits, or rather rare in combination: kindness, humour, curiosity, and a knowing brilliance, always offered as the mild gift of the moment, without competition or self-regard' – was inseparable from Ashbery the poet: 'he loved being here and was able somehow to translate his love of being here into language, directly, so that when you read his work you are reading *being alive*.'[2]

The channels and tributaries of Ashbery's afterlives run deep. Drawn to the local and the minor, he fashioned a whole new way

Ashbery receiving the Raymond Roussel Society Medal, June 2017.

of being a poet and a new poetic idiom, sometimes dissonant, sometimes synchronous, but always flexible; a poetic language that has proved irresistible to younger generations of poets. The urgencies of intimacy, the deflation of rhetoric, the resistance to violence and to power's multiform shapes, and the otherworldliness of pleasure are everywhere to be found in Ashbery's work; and there is, above all, a vigorous attachment to life.

The last poem he wrote, 'Climate Correction', which was circulated three weeks before his death in a 92Y Poetry tribute in December 2017, and later published in *Harper's*, articulates the urgency of his legacy distinctly as one of a foreclosed planetary futurity. The wager of the poem, as with all of Ashbery's poems, is the reader's own foibles: our own failure at clear-sightedness; our ability to be unfaithful to ourselves and to our desires. But it is also trusting of the intimacy held by its readership – of our capacity to go on surprising ourselves. The poems are, in this way, deeply hopeful in their unflinching reckoning with the present. Ashbery's cultural contributions are vast, and like his own archival production, not fully assimilable. But what is certain is that he has expanded our sense of how we might read and who, or what, the reader of poetry might be. 'As he said,' the poet Fred Moten writes, 'the poem is you, so he can't stop, which is wonderful.'[3]

References

Introduction: 'Everybody's Autobiography': Writing Against the Confessional Grain

1 Cited in David Orr and Dinita Smith, 'John Ashbery is Dead at 90: A Poetic Voice Often Echoed, Never Matched', *New York Times*, 3 September 2017.
2 John Ashbery, 'The Invisible Avant-Garde', in *Reported Sightings* (New York, 1989), pp. 389–95.
3 John Ashbery, *Your Name Here* (Manchester, 2000), p. 96; John Ashbery, *Collected Poems, 1956–1987*, ed. Mark Ford (Manchester, 2008).
4 Ibid., p. 487.
5 John Ashbery, 'Reading and Interview on *The Book Show*, 1992'.
6 John Ashbery, *Selected Prose*, ed. Eugene Richie (Manchester, 2004), p. 55.
7 John Ashbery, *Parallel Movement of the Hands* (New York, 2021), p. 29.
8 Ibid., p. 164.
9 Ibid., p. 81.
10 Deborah Nelson, *Pursuing Privacy in Cold War America* (New York, 2002), p. 12.
11 Sue Gangel, 'An Interview with John Ashbery', *San Francisco Review of Books*, III/7 (1977), reprinted in *American Poetry Observed: Poets on Their Work*, ed. Joe David Bellamy (Champaign, IN, 1984), p. 14.
12 Bryan Appleyard, 'The Major Genius of a Minor Art', *The Times*, www.carcanet.co.uk, 23 August 1984.
13 Ryan Ruby, 'The Irony of Fate', *The Nation*, 27 January 2002.
14 Adam Fitzgerald, 'A Refutation of Common Sense: An Interview with John Ashbery', www.bostonreview.net, 29 April 2011.
15 John Ashbery, 'An Interview with John Murphy', *Poetry Review*, LV/2 (1985), p. 25.

16 Paul de Man, 'Autobiography as De-Facement', *MLN*, XCIV/5 (1979),
    p. 921.
17 Gangel, 'An Interview with John Ashbery', p. 10.
18 John Ashbery, *Other Traditions* (Cambridge, MA, 2000), p. 104.
19 Ashbery, *Collected Poems, 1956–1987*, p. 496.
20 Marianne Moore, *The Poems of Marianne Moore*, ed. Grace Schulman
    (London, 2003), p. 141.
21 Ashbery, *Collected Poems, 1956–1987*, p. 492.
22 Ibid., p. 28.

1 'Living on the Edge of a Live Volcano': Childhood, 1927–42

1   Mark Ford, *John Ashbery in Conversation with Mark Ford* (London,
    2003), p. 22.
2   Ibid., p. 19.
3   Ibid., p. 20.
4   Ibid., p. 21.
5   John Ashbery, *Collected Poems, 1956–1987*, ed. Mark Ford (Manchester,
    2008), p. 9.
6   Ford, *John Ashbery in Conversation with Mark Ford*, p. 10.
7   Ashbery, *Collected Poems, 1956–1987*, p. 165.
8   James Schuyler, *Collected Poems* (New York, 1994), pp. 245–6.
9   Ford, *John Ashbery in Conversation with Mark Ford*, p. 22.
10 Ibid.
11 Ashbery, *Collected Poems, 1956–1987*, p. 501.
12 Cited in Karin Roffman, *The Songs We Know Best: John Ashbery's Early
    Life* (New York, 2017), p. 63.
13 Ashbery Papers, AM 6 Box 31.
14 Ashbery, *Collected Poems, 1956–1987*, p. 186.
15 John Ashbery, *Your Name Here* (Manchester, 2000), p. 3.
16 John Ashbery Papers, AM 6 Carton 28.
17 John Ashbery, 'The Poetic Medium of W. H. Auden', AM 6 Box 31, John
    Ashbery (JA) Papers, Houghton Library, Harvard University.
18 John Ashbery, *Pre-Deerfield Diary*, 22 September 1942, AM 6 Box 31,
    JA Papers.

19 Michael Leddy, 'Live and Art: John Ashbery and Henry Darger', *Jacket 2*, http://jacketmagazine.com, 17 June 2002.

20 Melanie Rehak, 'The Way We Live Now: 4-4-99-Questions for John Ashbery; A Child in Time', *New York Times*, www.nytimes.com, 4 April 2009.

21 John Ashbery, 'Cups with Broken Handles', AM6 Box 27, JA Papers.

22 Cited in Roffman, *The Songs We Know Best*, p. 45.

23 Ashbery, *Your Name Here*, p. 31.

24 Ashbery, *Collected Poems, 1956–1987*, p. 520.

25 Ibid., p. 520.

26 Ibid., p. 29.

27 Karin Roffman, 'Ashbery's Earliest Translations', *Farrar, Straus & Giroux Work-in-Progress*, https://fsgworkinprogress.com, April 2014.

28 Roffman, *The Songs We Know Best*, p. 74.

29 Ford, *John Ashbery in Conversation with Mark Ford*, p. 26.

30 Cited in Roffman, *The Songs We Know Best*, p. 75.

31 Ashbery, *Collected Poems, 1956–1987*, p. 14.

32 Roffman, *The Songs We Know Best*, p. 81.

33 Mark Ford, 'Letters: And So It Goes – Letters From Young Mr Grace (aka John Ashbery)', www.pnreview.co.uk, February 2018.

34 Ashbery, *Planisphere* (New York, 2009), p. 21.

35 Roffman, *The Songs We Know Best*, p. 97.

36 Ibid., p. 102.

2 'Our Days Put on Such Reticence': The Making of Little J. A., 1943–9

1 Mark Ford, *John Ashbery in Conversation with Mark Ford* (London, 2003), p. 28.

2 Karin Roffman, *The Songs We Know Best: John Ashbery's Early Life* (New York, 2017), p. 104.

3 Robert Gottlieb, 'My President', *New York Review of Books*, www.nybooks.com, 16 January 2010.

4 Cited in Roffman, *The Songs We Know Best*, p. 108.

5 Ibid., p. 105.

6 Letter from Frank Boyden to Chet Ashbery, 3 January 1944, AM6 Box 26, JA Papers.

7 Cited in Roffman, *The Songs We Know Best*, p. 119.

8 Ibid., p. 105.

9 Ibid., p. 136.

10 Ibid., p. 116.

11 Ibid., p. 109.

12 Ibid., p. 119.

13 John Ashbery, 'A Ride on the Bus', *Deerfield Scroll*, 27 January 1945, AM6 Box 27, JA Papers.

14 Roffman, *The Songs We Know Best*, p. 119.

15 Cited ibid., p. 110.

16 John Ashbery, *Collected Poems, 1956–1987*, ed. Mark Ford (Manchester, 2008), p. 889.

17 Cited in Roffman, *The Songs We Know Best*, p. 129.

18 Ibid., p. 121.

19 Ashbery, *Collected Poems, 1956–1987*, p. 889.

20 Ibid., p. 890.

21 John Ashbery, 'Why We Forget Our Dreams', AM6 Box 30, JA Papers.

22 Richard Kostelanetz, 'How to Be a Difficult Poet', *New York Times*, www.nytimes.com, 23 May 1976.

23 John Ashbery, 'Interview with David Lehman', 17 October 1977, AM6 Box 31, JA Papers.

24 John Ashbery, 'Recent Tendencies in Poetry', 13 February 1945, AM6 Box 31, JA Papers.

25 Cited in Roffman, *The Songs We Know Best*, p. 111.

26 Author interview with Trevor Winkfield, 28 November 2020.

27 Roffman, *The Songs We Know Best*, p. 131.

28 John Ashbery, 'Prayer', AM6 Box 28, JA Papers.

29 Paul Boyer, *By the Bomb's Early Light: American Thought and Culture at the Dawn of the Atomic Age* (Chapel Hill, NC, 1994), p. 7.

30 Andrew Epstein, *Beautiful Enemies: Friendship and Postwar American Poetry* (Oxford, 2006), p. 152.

31 Ashbery, *Collected Poems, 1956–1987*, p. 37.

32 Henry Rasof and Ellen Wisoff, 'An Interview with John Ashbery', *Modularist Review*, 2 (Summer 1976), p. 47.

33 Ashbery, 'Second Presentation of Elizabeth Bishop', in John Ashbery, *Selected Prose*, ed. Eugene Richie (Manchester, 2004), p. 164.

34 John Ashbery, 'W. H. Auden and Marianne Moore [College Paper]', F. O. Matthiessen, 20th C. Poetry, Spring 1949, AM6 Box 31, JA Papers.

35 Roffman, *The Songs We Know Best*, p. 184.

36 Cited ibid., p. 146.

37 John Ashbery and Ron Padgett, 'Oral History Initiative: On Frank O'Hara', Woodberry Poetry Room, www.youtube.com, accessed 15 November 2020.

38 Roffman, *The Songs We Know Best*, p. 154.

39 Ibid., p. 148.

40 Ashbery, *Collected Poems, 1956–1987*, p. 898.

41 Roffman, *The Songs We Know Best*, pp. 156–7.

42 John Ashbery, 'My Friends', AM6 Box 28, JA Papers.

43 Michel Foucault, 'Friendship as a Way of Life', in *Ethics, Subjectivity and Truth* (New York, 1997), pp. 136–40.

44 Roffman, *The Songs We Know Best*, p. 159.

45 Cited in Jenni Quilter, 'Explicit as a Star', *Poetry Magazine*, www.poetryfoundation.org, 16 December 2013.

46 Ashbery, *Collected Poems, 1956–1987*, p. 28.

47 Cited in Roffman, *The Songs We Know Best*, p. 164.

48 Sigmund Freud, *Standard Edition*, vol. IV, part 1: *The Interpretation of Dreams* (London, 2001), p. 47.

49 Roffman, *The Songs We Know Best*, p. 166.

50 Ibid., p. 169.

51 John Ashbery, 'W. H. Auden and Marianne Moore [College Paper]', JA Papers.

52 John Ashbery and Ron Padgett, 'Oral History Initiative: On Frank O'Hara', Woodberry Poetry Room, www.youtube.com, 26 January 2012.

53 Roffman, *The Songs We Know Best*, p. 176.

54 'Oral History Initiative: On Frank O'Hara'.

55 Ashbery, *Collected Poem, 1956–1987*, p. 890.

56 Ibid., p. 891.

57 Letter from John Ashbery to Jane Freilicher, 18 September 1950, Jane Freilicher (JF) Papers, Houghton Library.

3 'Excitation, Excitation of Feeling/ Excitement, Mental
Excitement': The Encouraging Climate of New York, 1949–55

1 Donald Allen, ed., *The Collected Poems of Frank O'Hara* (Berkeley,
   CA, 1995), p. 499.
2 Jenni Quilter, *New York School Painters and Poets: Neon in Daylight*
   (New York, 2014), p. 173.
3 John Ashbery, *Collected Poems, 1956–1987*, ed. Mark Ford (Manchester,
   2008), p. 905.
4 Postcard from John Ashbery to Jane Freilicher, 8 September 1950,
   JF Papers.
5 John Ashbery, 'Frank Lloyd Wright', in *Reported Sightings* (New York,
   1989), p. 321.
6 Ashbery, 'Poetical Space', in *Selected Prose*, ed. Eugene Richie
   (Manchester, 2004), p. 214.
7 Karin Roffman, *The Songs We Know Best: John Ashbery's Early Life*
   (New York, 2017), p. 181.
8 Ibid., p. 182.
9 Cited in Jenni Quilter, 'Explicit as a Star', *Poetry Magazine*, www.
   poetryfoundation.org, 16 December 2013.
10 Kenneth Koch, *The Collected Poems of Kenneth Koch* (New York, 2005),
   p. 461.
11 Cited in Quilter, 'Explicit as a Star'.
12 Dinitia Smith, 'Poem Alone', *New York Magazine*, 20 May 1991.
13 Roffman, *The Songs We Know Best*, p. 186.
14 Ashbery, *Collected Poems, 1956–1987*, p. 14.
15 Letter from John Ashbery to Richard Elliott, 17 September 1950,
   JA Papers.
16 John Ashbery Interview, AM6 Box 31, JA Papers.
17 Ashbery, *Collected Poems, 1956–1987*, p. 17.
18 Marianne Moore, 'New York', in *The Poems of Marianne Moore*,
   ed. Grace Schulman (London, 2003), p. 146.
19 Ashbery, *Collected Poem, 1956–1987*, p. 907.
20 Roffman, *The Songs We Know Best*, p. 182.
21 Ibid., p. 183.
22 Cited ibid., p. 184.
23 Ibid., p. 186.

24 John Ashbery, *Three Plays* (Calais, VT, 1978), pp. 3–7.

25 Letter from John Ashbery to Jane Freilicher, 1951, JF Papers.

26 Roffman, *The Songs We Know Best*, p. 194.

27 Cited ibid., p. 192.

28 John Ashbery, 'Introduction', *The Collected Poems of Frank O'Hara*, ed. Allen, p. viii.

29 Letter from John Ashbery to Jane Freilicher, 8 August 1950, JF Papers. Cited in Roffman, *The Songs We Know Best*, p. 192.

30 Cited ibid., p. 194.

31 Ibid., p. 195.

32 Letter from John Ashbery to Jane Freilicher, 12 July 1951, JF Papers, cited ibid., p. 197.

33 Ibid.

34 Roffman, *The Songs We Know Best*, p. 198.

35 Ashbery, *Reported Sightings*, p. 241.

36 Susan Sontag, 'Notes on Camp', in *Against Interpretation and Other Essays* (London, 2009), pp. 275–92.

37 Margot Canaday, *The Straight State: Sexuality and Citizenship in Twentieth-Century America* (Princeton, NJ, 2009), pp. 1–2.

38 Joseph LeSueur, *Digressions on Some Poems by Frank O'Hara* (New York, 2003), p. xiii.

39 Ashbery, *Collected Poems, 1956–1987*, p. 35.

40 James Schuyler, *Collected Poems* (New York, 1994), pp. 286–7.

41 Roffman, *The Songs We Know Best*, p. 215.

42 Marjorie Perloff, '"Transparent Selves": The Poetry of Frank O'Hara and John Ashbery', *Yearbook of English Studies*, VIII (1978), p. 173.

43 Roffman, *The Songs We Know Best*, p. 194.

44 Ashbery, *Collected Poems, 1956–1987*, p. 21.

45 Ibid., pp. 14–15; Letter from O'Hara to Larry Rivers, 30 December 1952, Box 11, Folder 7, Larry Rivers (LR) Papers.

46 Roffman, *The Songs We Know Best*, p. 223.

47 Ibid., p. 203.

48 Ibid., p. 229.

49 Ibid., p. 23.

50 Ibid., p. 12.

51 Richard Kostelanetz, 'How to Be a Difficult Poet', *New York Times*, www.nytimes.com, 23 May 1976.

52 Roffman, *The Songs We Know Best*, p. 230.

53 Margaret Carson, 'Eugene Richie and Rosanne Wasserman on John Ashbery's *Collected French Translations*', *wwb Daily*, 15 February 2017.

54 Roffman, *The Songs We Know Best*, p. 233.

55 Rosanne Wasserman and Eugene Richie, '"All the Things One Wants:" John Ashbery's French Translation', *Massachusetts Review*, LIV/4 (2013), p. 595.

56 John Ashbery, *Selected Prose*, ed. Eugene Richie (Manchester, 2004), p. 45.

57 Letter from Frank O'Hara to Larry Rivers, 28 April 1955, Box 11, Folder 8, LR Papers.

58 Cited in John Emil Vincent, *John Ashbery and You: His Later Books* (Athens, GA, 2007), pp. 1–2.

59 W. H. Auden, 'Foreword' to John Ashbery, *Some Trees* (New Haven, CT, 1956), p. 16.

60 Letter from John Ashbery to Jane Freilicher, 1 September 1960, JF Papers.

61 Letter from Ashbery to Freilicher, 9 December 1955, Jane Freilicher Papers, MS Am 2072 (2).

62 Grace Hartigan, *The Journals of Grace Hartigan, 1951–1955*, ed. William T. La Moy and Joseph P. McCaffrey (Syracuse, NY, 2009), p. 183.

63 Ibid., p. 177.

64 Ibid., p. 178.

65 Ibid., p. 179.

66 Roffman, *The Songs We Know Best*, p. 230.

67 Ibid., p. 233.

68 Ashbery, *Collected Poems, 1956–1987*, p. 6.

69 Hartigan, *The Journals of Grace Hartigan, 1951–1955*, p. 178.

70 Roffman, *The Songs We Know Best*, p. 239.

4 'I Love Trashy Things as Long as They're French': Taking French Leave, 1955–64

1 Henri Lefebvre, *Critique of Everyday Life*, vol. I, trans. John Moore (London, 1991), p. 231.

2 Michel Aglietta, *A Theory of Capitalist Regulation: The U.S. Experience* (London, 2000), p. 159.

3   Letter from Ashbery to Freilicher, 9 December 1955, Jane Freilicher Papers, MS Am 2072 (2).

4   Mark Ford, *John Ashbery in Conversation with Mark Ford* (London, 2003), p. 41.

5   Daniel Kane, 'Reading John Ashbery's *The Tennis Court Oath* through Man Ray's Eye', *Textual Practice*, XXI/3 (2007), p. 553.

6   Ibid., p. 560.

7   Georges Perec, *Things: A Story of the Sixties with a Man Asleep*, trans. David Bellos (London, 2011), p. 55.

8   Ashbery Papers, AM 6 Carton 25 of 56.

9   Perec, *Things*, p. 190.

10 Ibid., p. 71.

11 Hélène Cardona, 'Interview with American Wordsmith (and Poet), the late John Ashbery', Wordsmiths Blog, www.wordsmithsblog.com, 5 December 2019.

12 John Ashbery, 'Introduction' to Pierre Martory, *The Landscapist Is Behind the Door*, trans. John Ashbery (Riverdale-on-Hudson, NY, 1994), p. x.

13 Ford, *John Ashbery in Conversation with Mark Ford*, p. 40.

14 Martory, *The Landscapist Is Behind the Door*, p. 85.

15 Cited in Adam Thorpe, 'Review: The Landscapist – Selected Poems by Pierre Martory', *The Guardian*, www.theguardian.com, 24 October 2008.

16 Martory, *The Landscapist Is Behind the Door*, p. 29.

17 Ibid., p. ix.

18 John Ashbery, *Collected Poems, 1956–1987*, ed. Mark Ford (Manchester, 2008), p. 44.

19 Ford, *John Ashbery in Conversation with Mark Ford*, p. 48.

20 Letter from Ashbery to Jane Freilicher, 8 September 1960, JF Papers.

21 Ibid., p. 49.

22 Richard Kostelanetz, 'How to Be a Difficult Poet', *New York Times*, www.nytimes.com, 23 May 1976.

23 Letter from John Ashbery to James Schuyler, 21 February 1960, James Schuyler (JS) Papers, University of California at San Diego.

24 Letter from John Ashbery to James Schuyler, 9 August 1959, JS Papers.

25 Letter from John Ashbery to James Schuyler, 28 December 1959, JS Papers.

26 Letter from Ashbery to Freilicher, 9 December 1955, Jane Freilicher Papers, MS Am 2072 (2); and see Ashbery, *Collected Poems, 1956–1987*, pp. 61–2.

27 John Ash, 'In Conversation with John Ashbery', *PN Review*, XII/2 (November–December 1985), pp. 31–5.

28 Ford, *John Ashbery in Conversation with Mark Ford*, p. 44.

29 Ibid., p. 44.

30 Letter from Frank O'Hara to John Ashbery, 22 December 1958, Frank O'Hara (FOH) Papers.

31 Letter from Frank O'Hara to John Ashbery, 26 January 1959, FOH Papers.

32 Letter from Frank O'Hara to John Ashbery, 14 July 1959, FOH Papers.

33 A. Poulin Jr, 'The Experience of Experience: A Conversation with John Ashbery', *Michigan Quarterly Review*, XX/3 (1981), pp. 250–51.

34 Ashbery, *Collected Poems, 1956–1987*, p. 64.

35 Ashbery Papers, AM 6 Carton 25 of 56.

36 Ford, *John Ashbery in Conversation with Mark Ford*, p. 43.

37 John Ashbery, *Reported Sightings* (New York, 1989), p. 87.

38 Ibid., pp. 87–8.

39 Ibid., p. 92.

40 Ibid., p. 109.

41 Ibid.

42 Ford, *John Ashbery in Conversation with Mark Ford*, p. 43.

43 Ibid., p. 47.

44 John Ashbery, *Selected Prose*, ed. Eugene Richie (Manchester, 2004), p. 250.

45 Ibid.

46 Ibid.

47 Ibid.

48 Ibid., p. 251.

49 Ibid.

50 Ashbery, *Collected Poems, 1956–1987*, p. 92.

51 Bill Berkson, 'Code Unknown: John Ashbery', *Poetry Magazine*, www.poetryfoundation.org, 3 April 2013.

52 Letter from Frank O'Hara to John Ashbery, 7 January 1960, FOH Papers.

53 Ashbery, *Selected Prose*, p. 67.

54 Ibid.

55 William Packard, ed., *The Poet's Craft: Interviews from The New York Quarterly* (New York, 1987), p. 83.

56 Ashbery, *Collected Poems, 1956–1987*, p. 103.

57 Ashbery, *Reported Sightings*, p. 17.

58 John Ashbery, 'In Conversation with John Tranter' [20 April 1985], *Jacket 2*, http://jacketmagazine.com.

59 Ford, *John Ashbery in Conversation with Mark Ford*, p. 44.

60 Pierre Restany, excerpts from 'À Quarante Degrés au-dessus de dada' [May 1961], in *Le Nouveau Réalisme*, trans. Martha Nichols (Paris, 1978), pp. 281–5.

61 Ibid., p. 66.

62 Ashbery, *Reported Sightings*, p. 114.

63 John Ashbery, 'Larry Rivers Was Dying: He Asked to See Friends', *New York Times*, www.nytimes.com, 25 August 2002.

64 Ashbery, *Reported Sightings*, p. 82.

65 Ibid.

66 Ibid.

67 Ashbery, *Collected Poems, 1956–1987*, p. 118.

68 Ibid., p. 43.

69 Cited in Mark Ford, 'Review of Pierre Martory's *The Landscapist*', *TLS*, 13 March 2008.

70 Thomas Crow, 'Patriotism and Virtue: David to the Young Ingres', in Stephen F. Eisenman, *Nineteenth Century Art: A Critical History* (London, 1994), p. 31.

71 Ford, *John Ashbery in Conversation with Mark Ford*, p. 46.

72 Ibid.

73 John Ashbery, 'In Conversation with John Tranter' [May 1988], *Jacket 2*, http://jacketmagazine.com.

74 Cited in John Shoptaw, *On the Outside Looking Out* (Cambridge, MA, 1994), p. 94.

75 Richard Kostelanetz, 'How to Be a Difficult Poet', *New York Times*, www.nytimes.com, 23 May 1976.

76 Ashbery, *Collected Poems, 1956–1987*, p. 152.

77 Author interview with Trevor Winkfield, 25 November 2020.

78 Ibid., p. 171.

5 'The Invisible Avant-Garde': Turning Down Warhol, 1965–75

1 Author interview with Ron Padgett, 22 November 2020.

2 Author interview with Trevor Winkfield, 25 November 2020.

3 For the 'amusing intricate rules', see David Lehamn, *The Last Avant-Garde: The Making of the New York School Poets* (New York, 1999), p. 84. See John Ashbery and Kenneth Koch, *Locus Solus II* (Lans-en-Vercors, 1961).

4 Author interview with Ron Padgett, 22 November 2020.

5 For the title poem, see John Ashbery, *Collected Poems, 1956–1987*, ed. Mark Ford (Manchester, 2008), p. 127; Letter from Ashbery to Kenward Elmslie and Joe Brainard, 22 August 1970, Kenward Elmslie Papers, MSS 0521, UCSD, Box 1, Folder 22. On 'These Lacustrine Cities', see John Ashbery in Conversation with Bruce Kawin, WKCR Radio, 5 May 1966.

6 Ibid.

7 Ibid.

8 Ashbery, *Collected Poems, 1956–1987*, p. 129.

9 Ibid., p. 139.

10 Ibid., p. 135.

11 Richard Kostelanetz, 'How to Be a Difficult Poet', *New York Times*, www.nytimes.com, 23 May 1976.

12 John Koethe, 'On John Ashbery' and 'Short Takes on Long Poems', http://atlengthmag.com, accessed 14 October 2022.

13 Ashbery, *Collected Poems, 1956–1987*, p. 144.

14 John Ashbery, 'John Ashbery in Conversation with Harry Mathews', *Review of Contemporary Fiction*, VII/3 (Fall 1987), pp. 36–48.

15 Ibid.

16 Mark Ford, *John Ashbery in Conversation with Mark Ford* (London, 2003), p. 149.

17 Ibid., p. 50.

18 John Ashbery, *Reported Sightings* (New York, 1989), p. 390.

19 Ibid., p. 394.

20 Ford, *John Ashbery in Conversation with Mark Ford*, p. 51.

21 Ibid.

22 John Ash, 'In Conversation with John Ashbery', *PN Review*, XII/2 (November–December 1985).

23 Ford, *John Ashbery in Conversation with Mark Ford*, p. 52.

24 Ash, 'In Conversation with John Ashbery'.

25 Ashbery, *Reported Sightings*, p. 120.

26 Ibid., pp. 120–21.

27 Tony Scherman and David Dalton, *Pop: The Genius of Andy Warhol* (New York, 2009), p. 325.

28 Tom Clark and Lewis Warsh, 'To John Ashbery', in *Angel Hair Sleeps with a Boy in My Head: The Angel Hair Anthology*, ed. Anne Waldman et al. (New York, 2007), p. 278.

29 Ford, *John Ashbery in Conversation with Mark Ford*, p. 52.

30 Ibid.

31 Ashbery, 'Jane Freilicher', in *Reported Sightings*, p. 241.

32 John Ashbery, *Selected Prose*, ed. Eugene Richie (Manchester, 2004), p. 78.

33 Ibid.

34 Ibid., p. 211.

35 Ashbery, *Selected Prose*, p. 174.

36 Ibid.

37 Edmund White, *City Boy: My Life in New York During the 1960s and 1970s* (New York, 2009), p. 90.

38 Ashbery, *Collected Poems, 1956–1987*, p. 181.

39 Ashbery, *Selected Prose*, p. 90.

40 Ashbery, *Collected Poems, 1956–1987*, p. 206.

41 John Ashbery and Kenneth Koch, 'Death Paints a Picture' [1958], *artNews*, www.artnews.com, 9 January 2018.

42 John Ashbery, 'Interview by David Kermani', 2 June 1974, Oral History Collection, Columbia University.

43 Ashbery, *Collected Poems, 1956–1987*, p. 206.

44 Ibid., p. 184.

45 Ibid., p. 186.

46 See 'Alex Katz Remembers John Ashbery', www.phaidon.com, accessed 13 October 2022.

47 Ibid., p. 229.

48 Ibid., p. 232.

49 Ibid., p. 243.

50 Ford, *John Ashbery in Conversation with Mark Ford*, p. 52.

51 L. S. Asekoff, 'His Brooklyn College Years: Remembering John Ashbery', *Bomb*, www.bombmagazine.com, 8 September 2017.

52 Ross Labrie, 'John Ashbery: An Interview with Ross Labrie', *American Poetry Review*, XIII/13 (1984), p. 31.

53 Ford, *John Ashbery in Conversation with Mark Ford*, p. 56.

54 Richard Howard, 'Pursuits and Followings' [August 1972], *Poetry Magazine*, www.poetryfoundation.com.

55 Letter from Ashbery to Kenward Elmslie and Joe Brainard, 8 June and 14 July 1971, Kenward Elmslie Papers, MSS 0521, UCSD, Box 1, Folder 22

56 Larissa MacFarquhar, 'Present Waking Life: Becoming John Ashbery', *New Yorker*, www.newyorker.com, 7 November 2005.

57 Letter from John Ashbery to James Schuyler, 30 June 1970, James Schuyler (JS) Papers.

58 Letter from John Ashbery to James Schuyler, 16 December 1968, JS Papers.

59 Douglas Crase, 'Driving by the Lake with John Ashbery', *LitHub*, https://lithub.com, 28 October 2020.

60 Gerard Malanga, 'A Brief Encounter with John Ashbery', 1 January 2021, *Gerard Malanga Official*, https://gerardmalangaofficial.com.

61 Crase, 'Driving by the Lake with John Ashbery'.

62 John Tranter, 'Three John Ashberys' [1998], *Jacket 2*, http://jacketmagazine.com.

63 MacFarquhar, 'Present Waking Life: Becoming John Ashbery'.

64 Ash, 'In Conversation with John Ashbery'.

65 Edmund White, 'Why Can't We Stop Talking about New York in the Late 1970s?', *New York Times*, www.nytimes.com, 10 September 2015.

66 Sue Gangel, 'An Interview with John Ashbery' (originally printed in the *San Francisco Review of Books* (November 1977), reprinted in *American Poetry Observed: Poets On Their Work*, ed. Joe David Bellamy (Urbana, IL, 1984), p. 15.

67 Letter from Ashbery to Joe Brainard, 27 June 1974 and 4 August 1975, Joe Brainard Papers MSS 0703, Box 1, Folder 5.

68 Ashbery, *Collected Poems, 1956–1987*, p. 353.

69 Letter from Ashbery to Kenward Elmslie, 23 July 1974, Kenward Elmslie Papers, MSS 0521, UCSD, Box 1, Folder 22. Sue Gangel, 'An Interview with John Ashbery', *San Francisco Review of Books*, III/7 (1977), reprinted in *American Poetry Observed: Poets on Their Work*, ed. Joe David Bellamy (Champaign, IN, 1984), p. 11.

70 John Ashbery, 'A Man of Words', *Poetry*, November 1973.

71 Ashbery, *Collected Poems, 1956–1987*, p. 401.

72 Andrew Strombeck, *DIY on the Lower East Side: Books, Buildings, and Art After the 1975 Fiscal Crisis* (New York, 2020), pp. 29–30.

73 Ashbery, *Collected Poems, 1956–1987*, p. 480.

6 'I'm Famous for Being Famous': The Decade of Self-Inventiveness, 1975–84

1 Edmund White, *City Boy: My Life in New York During the 1960s and 1970s* (New York, 2009), p. 91.

2 David Lehman, 'The Pleasures of Poetry', *New York Times Magazine*, 16 December 1984.

3 John Ashbery, *Collected Poems, 1956–1987*, ed. Mark Ford (Manchester, 2008), p. 477.

4 Ibid., pp. 475–6.

5 Rich Kelley, 'The Library of America Interviews John Ashbery', www. loa.org, 2 October 2008.

6 Richard Kostelanetz, 'How to Be a Difficult Poet', *New York Times*, www.nytimes.com, 23 May 1976.

7 Ashbery, *Collected Poems, 1956–1987*, p. 474.

8 Ibid., p. 486.

9 Kelley, 'The Library of America Interviews: John Ashbery', p. 4.

10 Ibid.

11 Ibid.

12 Wayne Koestenbaum, *Andy Warhol: A Biography* (New York, 2001), p. 179.

13 John Ash, 'In Conversation with John Ashbery', *PN Review*, XII/2 (November–December 1985).

14 Ashbery, *Collected Poems, 1956–1987*, p. 484.

15 Ibid., pp. 436–40.

16 Ibid., pp. 252–3.

17 Ibid., p. 282.

18 Letter from Ashbery to Elmslie, 17 September 1974, Elmslie Papers. Daniel Kane, 'Interview with John Ashbery' (1988), The Centre for Programs in Creative Writing, https://writing.upenn.edu.

19 Ashbery, *Collected Poems, 1956–1987*, p. 520.

20 Ibid., p. 499.

21 L. S. Asekoff, 'His Brooklyn College Years: Remembering John Ashbery', *Bomb*, www.bombmagazine.com, 8 September 2017.

22 Kate Guadagnino and Thessaly La Force, eds, 'What New York Was Like in the Early '80s – Hour by Hour', *New York Times*, www.nytimes.com, 17 April 2018.

23 Author interview with Trevor Winkfield, 25 November 2020.

24 Kostelanetz, 'How to Be a Difficult Poet'.

25 Ashbery, *Collected Poems, 1956–1987*, p. 482.

26 Dinitia Smith, 'Poem Alone', *New York Magazine*, 20 May 1991.

27 Ashbery, *Collected Poems, 1956–1987*, p. 486.

28 Ibid., p. 512.

29 Mark Ford, *John Ashbery in Conversation with Mark Ford* (London, 2003), p. 58.

30 Ibid., pp. 58–9.

31 Ashbery, *Collected Poems, 1956–1987*, p. 510.

32 Ibid., p. 511.

33 Cited in Jeffrey Gray, *Mastery's End: Travel and Postwar American Poetry* (Athens, GA, and London, 2005), p. 258.

34 Elizabeth Bishop, *Complete Poems* (London, 2004), p. 164.

35 Letter from Elizabeth Bishop to John Ashbery, 5 March 1973, Elizabeth Bishop Papers 1.6, Vassar Archives and Special Collections Library.

36 John Ashbery, *Selected Prose*, ed. Eugene Richie (Manchester, 2004), p. 120.

37 Ashbery, *Collected Poem, 1956–1987*, p. 495.

38 Ibid., p. 496.

39 Ibid., pp. 496–7.

40 John Ashbery, *Reported Sightings* (New York, 1989), p. 300.

41 Ford, *John Ashbery in Conversation with Mark Ford*, pp. 61–2.

42 Smith, 'Poem Alone'.

43 Ford, *John Ashbery in Conversation with Mark Ford*, p. 62.

44 Benjamin Moser, *Sontag: Her Life* (London, 2019), pp. 41–2.

45 Piotr Summer, 'John Ashbery', in *Code of Signals: Recent Writing in Poetics*, ed. Michael Palmer (Berkeley, CA, 1983), p. 313.

46 Ibid., p. 299.

47 Ford, *John Ashbery in Conversation with Mark Ford,* p. 60.

48 Kelley, 'The Library of America Interviews: John Ashbery'.

49 Ford, *John Ashbery in Conversation with Mark Ford,* p. 60.

50 Ann Lauterbach, 'What We Know as We Know It: Reading "Litany" with J. A.' [1979], *Conjunctions,* www.conjunctions.com.

51 Larissa MacFarquhar, 'Present Waking Life: Becoming John Ashbery', *New Yorker,* www.newyorker.com, 7 November 2005.

52 Ashbery, *Collected Poems, 1956–1987,* p. 672.

53 Ford, *John Ashbery in Conversation with Mark Ford,* p. 64.

54 Ibid.

55 Ash, 'In Conversation with John Ashbery'.

56 The interior of the house can be seen in 360 degrees in Yale's digital project 'John Ashbery's Nest', http://vr.ashberyhouse.yale.edu, accessed 10 April 2022.

57 Author interview with Trevor Winkfield, 25 November 2020.

58 Robert Harbison, *Eccentric Spaces* (Cambridge, MA, 1977), p. 63.

59 See https://dhlab.yale.edu/projects/nest.

60 MacFarquhar, 'Present Waking Life'.

61 John Koethe, 'An Interview with John Ashbery', *SubStance,* XI–XII/37–8 (1982–3), p. 184.

62 Richard Jackson, *Acts of Mind: Conversations with Contemporary Poets* (Tuscaloosa, AL, and London, 1983), p. 75.

63 Guadagnino and La Force, eds, 'What New York Was Like in the Early '80s – Hour by Hour'.

64 Ashbery, *Collected Poems, 1956–1987,* p. 703.

65 Ibid., p. 708.

66 Ibid., p. 709.

67 Ibid., p. 698.

68 John Shoptaw, *On the Outside Looking Out* (Cambridge, MA, 1994), p. 255.

69 Ashbery, *Collected Poems, 1956–1987,* p. 710.

70 Cited in Dennis Altman, *The Homosexualization of America: The Americanization of the Homosexual* (New York, 1982), p. 9.

71 Ashbery, *Collected Poems, 1956–1987,* p. 702.

72 Ibid., p. 720.

73 Ash, 'In Conversation with John Ashbery'.

7 'The Tribe of John': In the Manner of Ashbery, 1984–94

1 John Ashbery, *Collected Poems, 1956–1987*, ed. Mark Ford (Manchester, 2008), p. 787.

2 John Ashbery, 'In Conversation with John Tranter' [May 1988], *Jacket 2*, http://jacketmagazine.com.

3 Cited in Jay Parini, ed., *The Columbia History of American Poetry* (New York, 1993), p. 554.

4 Ashbery, *Collected Poems, 1956–1987*, pp. 791–2.

5 Cited in John Shoptaw, *On the Outside Looking Out* (Cambridge, MA, 1994), p. 275.

6 Ashbery, *Collected Poems, 1956–1987*, p. 787.

7 Author interview with Marjorie Perloff, 3 December 2020.

8 Ashbery, *Collected Poems, 1956–1987*, p. 804.

9 John Ashbery, 'John Ashbery in Conversation with David Remnick' [1980], *Bennington Review*, www.benningtonreview.org, 25 June 2020.

10 John Ashbery, *Selected Prose*, ed. Eugene Richie (Manchester, 2004), p. 62.

11 Ashbery, *Collected Poems, 1956–1987*, p. 742.

12 Jacques Lacan, *The Seminar of Jacques Lacan*, Book XVII: *The Other Side of Psychoanalysis*, ed. Jacques-Alain Miller, trans. Russell Grigg (New York and London, 2007), p. 14.

13 Cited in James Fenton, 'Getting Rid of the Burden of Sense', *New York Times*, www.nytimes.com, 29 December 1985.

14 Lee Harwood, *Collected Poems* (Exeter, 2004), p. 28.

15 Cited in Oli Hazzard, *John Ashbery and Anglo-American Exchange: The Minor Eras* (Oxford, 2018), p. 179.

16 Ashbery, *Collected Poems, 1956–1987*, p. 824.

17 David Bergman, 'The Queer Writer in New York', in *The Cambridge Companion to Gay and Lesbian Writing*, ed. Hugh Stevens (Cambridge, 2011), p. 230.

18 Ashbery, *Collected Poems, 1956–1987*, p. 846.

19 Author interview with Marjorie Perloff, 3 December 2020.

20 John Ashbery, ed., *The Best American Poetry 1988* (New York, 1988), p. xxiv.

21 Ashbery, 'John Ashbery in Conversation with John Tranter'.

22 Author interview with Trevor Winkfield, 4 December 2020; Mark Ford, *John Ashbery in Conversation with Mark Ford* (London, 2003), p. 64.

23 John Ashbery, *Flow Chart* (Manchester, 1991), p. 30.

24 Jenni Quilter, '"We even imagined the Posters": Collaborations between John Ashbery, Harry Mathews and Trevor Winkfield', *Word and Image*, xxv/2 (2009), p. 197.

25 John Ashbery, *Reported Sightings* (New York, 1989), pp. 170–72.

26 Dinitia Smith, 'Poem Alone', *New York Magazine*, 20 May 1991.

27 Sue Gangel, 'An Interview with John Ashbery', *San Francisco Review of Books*, iii/7 (1977), reprinted in *American Poetry Observed: Poets on Their Work*, ed. Joe David Bellamy (Champaign, in, 1984), p. 10.

28 Mark Ford, 'Letters: And So It Goes – Letters From Young Mr Grace (aka John Ashbery)', *pn Review* (February 2018).

29 Ashbery, *Selected Prose*, p. 214.

30 John Ashbery, 'Introduction' to Robert Mapplethorpe, *Pistils* (London, 1996), p. 6.

31 John Ashbery, *Other Traditions* (Cambridge, ma, 2000), p. 1.

32 Ibid., p. 70.

33 Ford, *John Ashbery in Conversation with Mark Ford*, p. 64.

34 Ashbery, *Flow Chart*, p. 27.

35 Ibid., p. 23.

36 Ibid., p. 216.

37 Author interview with Marjorie Perloff, 3 December 2020.

38 Ashbery, *Flow Chart*, p. 24.

39 Ibid., p. 186.

40 Ibid., p. 133.

41 Charles Bernstein, 'In the Wild: Remembering John Ashbery', *Bomb*, 8 September 2017.

42 Ashbery, *Flow Chart*, p. 34.

43 Ibid., p. 35.

44 Ibid., p. 134.

45 Ibid., p. 135.

46 John Ashbery, 'Guest Speaker: John Ashbery – The Poet's Hudson River Restoration', *Architectural Digest* (June 1994), p. 44.

47 Ford, 'Letters: And So It Goes'.

48 John Ashbery, 'In Conversation with David Herd', *pn Review* 99, xxi/1 (1996), p. 35.

49 John Ashbery, *Collected Poems, 1991–2000*, ed. Mark Ford (New York, 2017), p. 227.

50 Ashbery, *Selected Prose*, p. 223.

51 Ashbery, *Collected Poems, 1991–2000*, p. 346.

52 John Kinsella, 'Interview with John Tranter', 1991–1997, The Centre for Programs on Contemporary Writing, https://writing.upenn.edu.

53 Author interview with Marjorie Perloff, 3 December 2020.

54 Ashbery, *Collected Poems, 1991–2000*, p. 351.

55 Ibid., pp. 418–19.

56 Ibid., p. 383.

57 Ashbery, 'Guest Speaker: John Ashbery – The Poet's Hudson River Restoration', p. 44.

8 'Jump-Start Variety': The Zaniness of the Late Style, 1994–2017

1 John Ashbery, 'John Ashbery in Conversation with Harry Mathews', *Review of Contemporary Fiction*, VII/3 (Fall 1987), pp. 36–48.

2 John Ashbery, *Collected Poems, 1991–2000*, ed. Mark Ford (New York, 2017), p. 499.

3 Elizabeth Bishop, *Prose*, ed. Lloyd Schwartz (London, 2011), p. 331.

4 Ibid., p. 567.

5 John Ashbery, *Reported Sightings* (New York, 1989), p. 343.

6 Cited in David Herd, *John Ashbery and American Poetry* (Manchester, 2000), p. 2.

7 Ashbery, *Collected Poems, 1991–2000*, p. 580.

8 Sandra Simonds, 'Running into Capitalism: John Ashbery's "Girls on the Run", *Jacket 2*, http://jacketmagazine.com, 12 February 2018.

9 Melanie Rehak, 'The Way We Live Now: 4-4-99-Questions for John Ashbery; A Child in Time', *New York Times* (4 April 1999).

10 See Helen Vendler, 'John Ashbery, Toying with Words', *New York Times*, www.nytimes.com, 8 December 2009; Adam Phillips, 'Master of the Nonsensical', *The Guardian*, www.theguardian.com, 30 December 2007.

11 Marjorie Perloff, 'Still Time for Surprises', *Thumbscrew*, 18 (Spring 2001), pp. 46–8.

12 John Ashbery, *Chinese Whispers* (Manchester, 2002), p. 99.

13 John Ashbery, *Selected Prose*, ed. Eugene Richie (Manchester, 2004), p. 233.

14 John Ashbery, *Where Shall I Wander* (Manchester, 2005), p. 36.

15 Author interview with Marjorie Perloff, 3 December 2020.

16 John Ashbery, *A Worldly Country* (Manchester, 2007), p. 1.

17 John Ashbery, 'Barbara Epstein (1928–2006)', *New York Review of Books*, www.nybooks.com, 10 August 2006.

18 Ashbery, *Selected Prose*, p. 21.

19 Cited in Dan Piepenbring, 'Gluey and Scissory', *Paris Review*, www.theparisreview.org, 18 June 2015.

20 Author interview with Marjorie Perloff, 3 December 2020.

21 'Remembering John Ashbery: Writers Pay Tribute', www.loa.org, 1 September 2017.

22 Holland Cotter, 'The Poetry of Scissors and Glue', *New York Times*, www.nytimes.com, 12 September 2008.

23 Rich Kelley, 'The Library of America Interviews: John Ashbery', www.loa.org, 2 October 2008.

24 John Ashbery, *Planisphere* (New York, 2009), p. 128.

25 Ashbery, *Selected Prose*, pp. 149, 153, 299.

26 Spittle, 'Light Glyphs: John Ashbery'; John Ashbery, *Collected Poems, 1956–1987*, ed. Mark Ford (Manchester, 2008), p. 771.

27 Ashbery, *Collected Poems, 1956–1987*, p. 772.

28 Adam Fitzgerald, 'A Refutation of Common Sense: An Interview with John Ashbery', *Boston Review*, www.bostonreview.net, 29 April 2011.

29 Adam Fitzgerald, 'John Ashbery', *Interview*, www.interviewmagazine.com, 20 April 2015.

30 Darrel Alejandro Holnes, 'psa at the White House: On the 2011 National Medal of Arts and National Humanities Medal Ceremony', https://poetrysociety.org, 15 February 2012.

31 John Ashbery, *Quick Question* (Manchester, 2013), p. 67.

32 Ibid., p. 47.

33 Rosanne Wasserman, 'Hudson 1993: A Tour of John Ashbery's Home', *Rain Taxi*, www.raintaxi.com, March 2008.

34 Ibid.

35 Ben Lerner, 'The I and the You', *Paris Review*, www.theparisreview.org, 9 December 2015.

36 John Ashbery, *Breezeway* (Manchester, 2015), p. 61.

37 Ibid., p. 4.

38 'Biscuit Medal for John Ashbery', www.joanbofill.com, accessed 13 October 2022.

39 Author interview with Trevor Winkfield, 2 December 2020.

Epilogue: 'Let's Pay Attention': Ashbery's Afterlives

1 Lyn Hejinian, 'Tributes to John Ashbery', *Frieze*, www.frieze.com, 11 September 2017.

2 Amy King, 'And the Occasion Changed: A Tribute to John Ashbery', *Poetry Magazine*, www.poetryfoundation.com, 13 September 2017.

3 Ibid.

Bibliography

Allen, Donald, *The Collected Poems of Frank O'Hara*, ed. Donald Allen
 (Berkeley, CA, 1995)

Asekoff, L. S., 'His Brooklyn College Years: Remembering John Ashbery',
 Bomb, www.bombmagazine.com, 8 September 2017

Ash, John, 'In Conversation with John Ashbery', *PN Review*, XII/2
 (November–December 1985)

Ashbery, John, *Breezeway* (Manchester, 2015)

—, *Chinese Whispers* (Manchester, 2002)

—, *Collective French Translations*, ed. Rosanne Wasserman and Eugene
 Richie (New York, 2014)

—, *Collected Poems, 1956–1987*, ed. Mark Ford (Manchester, 2008)

—, *Collected Poems, 1991–2000*, ed. Mark Ford (New York, 2017)

—, *Commotion of the Birds* (Manchester, 2016)

—, *Flow Chart* (Manchester, 1991)

—, 'Interview by David Kermani', 2 June 1974, Oral History Collection,
 Columbia University

—, *Other Traditions* (Cambridge, MA, 2000)

—, *Parallel Movement of the Hands* (New York, 2021)

—, *Planisphere* (New York, 2009)

—, *Quick Question* (Manchester, 2013)

—, *Reported Sightings* (New York, 1989)

—, *Selected Prose*, ed. Eugene Richie (Manchester, 2004)

—, *Some Trees* (New Haven, CT, 1956)

—, *Three Plays* (Calais, VT, 1978)

—, *Where Shall I Wander* (Manchester, 2005)

—, *A Worldly Country* (Manchester, 2007)

—, *Your Name Here* (Manchester, 2000)

—, ed., *The Best American Poetry, 1988* (New York, 1988)

—, and Kenneth Koch, 'Death Paints a Picture' [1958], *ARTNews*, www. artnews.com, 9 January 2018

—, and Ron Padgett, 'Oral History Initiative: On Frank O'Hara', Woodberry Poetry Room, Harvard University, www.youtube.com, 26 January 2012

—, and James Schuyler, *A Nest of Ninnies* (New York, 2004)

Barthes, Roland, *Writing Degree Zero* (Paris, 1953)

Berkson, Bill, 'Code Unknown: John Ashbery', *Poetry Magazine*, www. poetryfoundation.com, 3 April 2013

Bishop, Elizabeth, *Complete Poems* (London, 2004)

Canaday, Margot, *The Straight State: Sexuality and Citizenship in Twentieth-Century America* (Princeton, NJ, 2009)

Cardona, Hélène, 'Interview with American Wordsmith (and Poet), the Late John Ashbery', Wordsmiths' Blog, wordsmithsblog.com, 5 December 2019

Delany, Samuel R., *Times Square Red, Times Square Blue* (New York and London, 1999)

de Man, Paul, 'Autobiography as De-Facement', *MLN*, XCIV/5 (1979), pp. 919–30

Epstein, Andrew, *Beautiful Enemies: Friendship and Postwar American Poetry* (Oxford, 2006)

Fitzgerald, Adam, 'A Refutation of Common Sense: An Interview with John Ashbery', *Boston Review*, 29 April 2011

Ford, Mark, *John Ashbery in Conversation with Mark Ford* (London, 2003)

—, 'Letters: And So It Goes – Letters From Young Mr Grace (aka John Ashbery)', *PN Review* (February 2018)

—, Review of Pierre Martory's *The Landscapist*, *TLS* (13 March 2008)

Fredman, Stephen, *Poet's Prose: The Crisis in American Verse* (Cambridge, 1983)

Gangel, Sue, 'An Interview with John Ashbery', *San Francisco Review of Books*, III/7 (1977), reprinted in *American Poetry Observed: Poets on their Work*, ed. Joe David Bellamy (Champaign, IN, 1984), pp. 9–19

Gooch, Brad, *City Poet: The Life and Times of Frank O'Hara* (New York, 2014)

Gray, Jeffrey, *Mastery's End: Travel and Postwar American Poetry* (Athens, GA, and London, 2005)

Harbison, Robert, *Eccentric Spaces* (Cambridge, MA, 1977)

Hartigan, Grace, *The Journals of Grace Hartigan, 1951–1955*, ed. William T. La Moy and Joseph P. McCaffrey (Syracuse, NY, 2009)

Hazzard, Oli, *John Ashbery and Anglo-American Exchange: The Minor Eras* (Oxford, 2018)

Herd, David, *John Ashbery and American Poetry* (Manchester, 2000)

Hickman, Ben, *John Ashbery and English Poetry* (Edinburgh, 2012)

Jackson, Richard, *Acts of Mind: Conversations with Contemporary Poets* (Tuscaloosa, AL, and London, 1983)

Kane, Daniel, 'Reading John Ashbery's *The Tennis Court Oath* through Man Ray's Eye', *Textual Practice*, XXI/3 (2007), pp. 551–75

Koethe, John, 'An Interview with John Ashbery', *SubStance*, XI–XII/37–8 (1982–3), pp. 178–86

—, 'On John Ashbery', in 'Short Takes on Long Poems, Volume 2', http://atlengthmag.com, accessed 10 August 2022

Kostelanetz, Richard, 'How to Be a Difficult Poet', *New York Times*, www.nytimes.com, 23 May 1976

Koestenbaum, Wayne, *Andy Warhol: A Biography* (New York, 2001)

Leddy, Michael, 'Live and Art: John Ashbery and Henry Darger', *Jacket 2*, http://jacketmagazine.com, 17 June 2002

Lefebvre, Henri, *Critique of Everyday Life*, vol. I, trans. John Moore (London, 1991)

Lehman, David, *The Last Avant-Garde: The Making of the New York School Poets* (New York, 1999)

Levy, Ellen, *Criminal Ingenuity: Moore, Cornell, Ashbery, and the Struggle Between the Arts* (Oxford, 2011)

Martory, Pierre, *The Landscapist Is Behind the Door* (Riverdale-on-Hudson, NY, 1994)

Moore, Marianne, *The Poems of Marianne Moore*, ed. Grace Schulman (London, 2003)

Myers, Bernard, *The Poets of the New York School* (Philadelphia, PA, 1969)

Nelson, Deborah, *Pursuing Privacy in Cold War America* (New York, 2002)

Orr, David, and Dinitia Smith, 'John Ashbery Is Dead at 90; A Poetic Voice Often Echoed, Never Matched', *New York Times*, www.nytimes.com, 3 September 2017

Packard, William, ed., *The Poet's Craft: Interviews from The New York Quarterly* (New York, 1987)

Perec, Georges, *Things: A Story of the Sixties with a Man Asleep*, trans. David Bellos (London, 2011)

Perloff, Marjorie, "'Transparent Selves': The Poetry of Frank O'Hara and John Ashbery', *Yearbook of English Studies*, VIII (1978), pp. 171–96

Quilter, Jenni, *New York School Painters and Poets: Neon in Daylight* (New York, 2014)

—, '"We even imagined the Posters": Collaborations between John Ashbery, Harry Mathews and Trevor Winkfield', *Word and Image*, XXV/2 (2009)

Rehak, Melanie, 'The Way We Live Now: 4-4-99-Questions for John Ashbery; A Child in Time', *New York Times*, www.nytimes.com, 4 April 1999

Roffman, Karin, *The Songs We Know Best: John Ashbery's Early Life* (New York, 2017)

Scherman, Tony, and David Dalton, *Pop: The Genius of Andy Warhol* (New York, 2009)

Simonds, Sandra, 'Running into Capitalism: John Ashbery's "Girls on the Run"', *Jacket 2*, http://jacketmagazine.com, 12 February 2018

Shaw, Lytle, *Frank O'Hara: The Poetics of Coterie* (Iowa City, IA, 2006)

Shoptaw, John, *On the Outside Looking Out* (Cambridge, MA, 1994)

Sontag, Susan, *Against Interpretation* (London, 2001)

Strombeck, Andrew, *DIY on the Lower East Side: Books, Buildings, and Art After the 1975 Fiscal Crisis* (New York, 2020)

Summer, Piotr, 'John Ashbery', in *Code of Signals: Recent Writing in Poetics*, ed. Michael Palmer (Berkeley, CA, 1983)

Tranter, John, 'Three John Ashberys' [1998], *Jacket 2*, http://jacketmagazine.com

Vincent, John Emil, *John Ashbery and You: His Later Books* (Athens, GA, 2007)

White, Edmund, *City Boy: My Life in New York During the 1960s and 1970s* (New York, 2009)

—, 'Why Can't We Stop Talking about New York in the Late 1970s?', *New York Times*, www.nytimes.com, 10 September 2015

Acknowledgements

No biography of John Ashbery would be possible without the ground-breaking work of Karin Roffman. This study is highly indebted to the breath-taking scope, rigour and generosity of her first volume of Ashbery's life and work. Mark Ford's conversation with Ashbery, and his exemplary scholarship on his work, has, too, been highly influential on the reading I present in these pages, as has David Herd's full-length study of Ashbery's work. I would like to extend my gratitude to David Lehman, Ron Padgett, Marjorie Perloff and Trevor Winkfield for taking the time to discuss Ashbery's work with me and for their illuminating insights into his work, and to Matthew Holman for discussions of Frank O'Hara's time in Europe. Thanks are owed, too, to Allison Chomet at the Fales Library, NYU; Emily Walhout and Mary Graham at Houghton Library, Harvard University; the archival team at Beinecke Library, Yale University; Jennifer Donovan and Heather Smedberg at UCSD; and Elisabeth Ivers, Ahndraya Parlato, Stephen Shore, Grant Delin and Joan Bofill for the provision of images during a pandemic.

Photo Acknowledgements

The author and publishers wish to express their thanks to the below sources of illustrative material and/or permission to reproduce it. Every effort has been made to contact copyright holders; should there be any we have been unable to reach or to whom inaccurate acknowledgements have been made please contact the publishers, and full adjustments will be made to any subsequent printings:

© 2020 The Andy Warhol Museum, Pittsburgh, PA, a museum of Carnegie Institute, all rights reserved, film still courtesy of The Andy Warhol Museum: p. 113; photo © 2017 Joan Bofill: p. 182; photo courtesy of Grant Delin: p. 178; Douglas Crase Papers, Beinecke Rare Book and Manuscript Library, Yale University, New Haven, CT, courtesy of Douglas Crase: p. 126; © Estate of Jane Freilicher/Eric Brown Art Group, private collection, photos courtesy of Kasmin Gallery, New York: pp. 67, 119; John Ashbery Collages, Beinecke Rare Book and Manuscript Library, Yale University, New Haven, CT, courtesy of Tibor de Nagy Gallery, New York, and David Kermani/ The Flow Chart Foundation, Hudson, NY: p. 47; John Ashbery Papers, Houghton Library, Harvard University, Cambridge, MA, courtesy of David Kermani/The Flow Chart Foundation, Hudson, NY: pp. 6, 22, 32, 37, 53, 83, 86, 98, 100; Jane Freilicher Papers, Houghton Library, Harvard University, Cambridge, MA, courtesy of Estate of Jane Freilicher: pp. 56, 71, 73, 109; Jane Freilicher Papers, Houghton Library, Harvard University, Cambridge, MA, courtesy of Estate of Jane Freilicher and David Kermani/The Flow Chart Foundation, Hudson, NY: pp. 65, 122, 125; Jane Freilicher Papers, Houghton Library, Harvard University, Cambridge, MA, courtesy of Clarice Rivers: p. 124; courtesy of David Kermani/The Flow Chart Foundation, Hudson, NY: p. 105; Larry Rivers Papers, Fales Library and Special Collections, New York University, courtesy of Larry Rivers Foundation: pp. 79, 144, 145; courtesy of Ron Padgett: p. 131; courtesy of Ahndraya Parlato: